Praise for Previous Volumes by David Adams

Where We Came In
 With extraordinary care, these poems fix and illuminate moments stolen from dreams and from the darkness of ordinary lives. Their emotional range is wide—from despair to humor to joy; their style invariability is graceful and assured.
 —Susan Hubbard, author of *A Season of Risks* (2010).

First Light
 David Adams is a true poet. Poem after poem treads meditatively across weather, music, Advent, a harbor, friends clasping hands in a highly visual language. *First Light* is engaging. Read it!
 —Mary Jarrell, author of *Remembering Randall* (1997) and
Jerome: The Biography of a Poem (1971).

Evidence of Love
 Evidence of love is illusive, but it is observed in what the lover sees and records in these poems of David Adams—elegant, elegiac, deeply imagined, meticulously crafted, gracefully phrased. "The mile markers pass like years" and tell us that "it's not just we who seem to shrink" and that "once we've waited long enough/hope is not so difficult to understand."
 —Herb Coursen, author of *Blues in the Night* (2010) and
Longfellow's Evangeline: An Adaptation in Modern Verse (2010).

Room for Darkness, Room for Light
 Who'd have dreamt that ordinary people—farmhands, factory workers, housewives—and familiar geography—the rustbelt Midwest, the stricken South, austere New England—could inspire such a treasury of wise and patient lyrics? David Adams has, and all of us are the better for it.
 —Robley Wilson, editor of *North American Review* (1969-2000),
author of *After Paradise* (2017).

LOOKING THE OTHER WAY

David Adams' *Looking the Other Way* is not merely a travel diary of Micronesia… it is, rather, an engagement with what Elizabeth Bishop calls "Questions of Travel,"—how our displacement through travel calls into question our very existence as we witness other ways of living. Adams' poems are suffused with loneliness, longing, and wisdom of quiet witness. These are poems that look and look again, the kind of looking that goes inwards as much as outward. Reading them, I'm reminded that attention itself is a kind of love.

—Philip Metres, author of *Shrapnel Maps* (2020) and
Pictures at an Exhibition: A Petersburg Album (2016).

WAITING PLACES

The apparent ease with which real American places (with their serendipitous Classical and Biblical names) and subjects (animals, parents, children, lovers) morph into symbols of the human desire for an answer to all that questions is a tribute to Adams' patient, careful eye, as he observes, looks inward, then upward to the stars.

—Suzanne Ferguson, editor of *Jarrell, Bishop, Lowell & Co.*
Middle Generation Poets in Context (2003).

HOPE
AS A
CONSTRUCTION:

NEW & SELECTED POEMS

BY
DAVID J. ADAMS

BOTTOM DOG PRESS
HARMONY SERIES

HURON, OHIO

Bottom Dog Press, Inc.
PO Box 425, Huron, OH 44839
Lsmithdog@aol.com
http://smithdocs.net

CREDITS:
General Editor: Larry Smith
Cover & Layout Design: Susanna Sharp-Schwacke
Cover Art: "At Nan Madol" by Floyd Takeuchi
Author Photograph: William Koeth
Title Page Photo: The Ohio Turnpike Viaduct. Cuyahoga Valley
National Park, Peninsula, OH. 2022. Photo by the author.

ACKNOWLEDGEMENTS:
A number of these poems appeared in earlier volumes of
mine, as well as in the memoir *Casual Labor*. I undertook serious
reflection and revision in making the selections here. Over the
years, many of these poems also appeared in a variety of journals
and anthologies, including the following: *Centennial Review, Edith
Chase Symposium Anthologies* (2020, '21, '22), *Gardenopolis, Heart-
lands, The Best of Heartlands, Kennebec, Hiram Poetry Review, Laurel
Review, North American Review, Off the Coast, Penumbra, Pudding
Magazine, The Listening Eye, Wolf Moon Poetry Press Journal*, et al.

Table of Contents

HOME COUNTRY

LOOKING AT A MAP OF THE MIDWEST INTERURBAN LINES

Flashed out like small veins
over the imaginable reductions of geography—
this heartland where the blood of progress
cast itself in steel: divisions, trunk lines,
villages flowering as circles and stars.

I look downward to these constellations.
Ohio is the dreamed connection:
silk dried as bright metal,
flamed interstices.

Lake Shore Electric, Cleveland & Southwestern,
Eastern Ohio, trace the placenames
of the old century for new meaning.
Lorain, Elyria, Bucyrus, Garrettsville.

There are no visible lives
in the map of the lines.

Those who hoped to go somewhere more quickly,
commerce and leisure at the same velocity,
sleep dreamless in the silent groves
I count in my own familiar spaces.

Ohio, I was born between these used up lines
and the map of visions
and missed the waves of possibility
as a kind of light with sparks
rolling out from the towns
to a slow, encumbered death.

The dreams were scattered in season
like your hardwood leaves—
the rights-of-way cutting the clay and shale
have inked themselves with their best ferocity
to what is left: the color of remembrance.

The locals, the expresses
that touched the slow lives of the riders
and passed to the salvage yards
are lost in the speed of dissolution,
the momentum of the years.

Looking at the map, looking at the lines,
I see the dead routes clustered in Ohio,
running off the page,
carving the white darkness.

Lake County

Dark beneath the sandy ridges,
beyond the steep, forested ravines
cutting the yellow shale like green serpents
eating rock, sinking deeper towards Erie,
deeper past the humus pits, past
the breaks of poplars and cottonwoods
to wind together as lagoons
swelling over the spits of brown sand
into the wide, green lake.

There are no counties as they were.
The white shacks with names like
Jolly Roger's or *The Captain's Head,*
with dusty lots where convertibles bred,
never offered their fish fries
along the routes that no one built.
No one lived through any war
and watched their dreams seeding
the square lawns of GI homes
like offspring diapered in cement.
No children, racing for something,
smashed their quick Fords into bridges.

No one shed their clothes in those ravines
and made love there, furtively,
listening for the crack of leaves.

Nor did the concretes ever bloom
the white, ribbonish dreams of the malls.
The sands and gravels were not quarried
into blinding hills. Nothing was zoned.
No one forgot a history because
there was nothing to remember,
and no one to remember it.

And no one could have seen it all
from water, on a foredeck, sunning,
staring through the glare, waiting
for the sun to redden the whole world,
to sink into a lake where everything
sinks deeper after some cold hunger,

rising for air
and there is no air.

A Woman in a Trailer Park

December's wind invades the office walls
at Robin's Trailer Park in Mantua, Ohio.
Inside, a woman rocks a cooing infant on her knee
and tells her mother in a single breath,
"Danny's getting out in two more weeks
an I ain't tol' him, I'm just scared."

The mother brushes ashes from her cigarette
across the rent receipts, her face as sallow
as a dirty sheet; she recites the litany
of *better do's* she knows from memory.
To watch this daughter is to understand
how none of this makes any difference more
than figuring the wind outside will come or go.
She knows what's coming is a granite falling
on her life, "It's my life now!"

The child softly clutches its way up
her sweater so that a nipple shows
so slightly through the purple yarns.
She does not move, and lets her own smoke
rise up as a history, drafting cross her eyes
that were a danger always, a robin's
bluest sky storming into violet,
grains of gold like distant lightning.

THREE SOLDIERS AT EUCLID BEACH: 1944

Buddies. In the photograph they are clustered
at a rail beneath the line of sycamores
that commands the beach. They seem
a size too small for their uniforms,
which hang on them like limp flags.
Their overseas caps are slanted near
their dark eyes. The chalky smiles
are difficult to gauge. A tall one points
toward the water, west. Long shadows.
In the background two girls walk away
showing their fat, white calves.
They are vague as the dark trees.

A Domestic Scene

Moonlight climbs above our headboard
to the wall, filtered through the lace
your mother gave. I lift my hands
in the speech we call *our whisper*,
and the words flutter like black doves
across the faded patterns of swans and reeds.

A friend asked me, "How do you talk to him
in the dark?" I wanted to say
your hands are like drunken geese
that learned to dance, and slowly,
slowly, got tired and settled
their way to words instead.
but for that we need the moon.

But for that I need to tell the truth
and never do even when I try.
I speak so quickly in the dark...
And your thick hands, with whom
my doves lie down these years upon
your thigh, have swallowed
everything I say. It's all right.

After twenty years, the shape of my heart
with you, what to shop for,
and where to go in August
are nearly the same shape.

It's as if each thought is held a moment
and then placed into the air.
It's all right even when, in the kitchen,
I must put down my cup and walk
around in front of you and still remember
the list of things I need to ask
and swallow those for which I have no signs.

Here in our darkness, my hands
are so free they don't know anything.
They just live. It's strange,
as I roll across your chest
and press your hands apart, to think
            "You talk too much."

A Gray Not Morning's Eye
—for Karen Gabay and Raymond Rodriquez

The light plant's useless stacks, as cold
as brick can lie, eclipse the grey lake sky.
A blur at first, a milky Eldorado
cuts me off and drags its snowy wake
across the Shoreway's broken lanes.
I watch the taillights shrink
to red illusions while the winds
reverberate as lines you burned
upon the insubstantial air still warm.

To have wished a darkness to be endless
was just to breathe the candled atmosphere
in which you met your eyes
and let your hands descend to pry apart
the world we shared with no escape,
Verona spilling ripe as plague.

Slowly, impossibly, you wound yourselves
into a single flower petaled with a wish
the light reproved. As if tethered in a gale
you did extend the frenzy of your fall
still flower to the end.

Your eyes' unbearable surprise
bleeds into this darkness that I drive,
where hearts still wake a dagger's inch
beyond the hope that knows full well
where it should be. And there it is.

A Nurse at the Frozen Foods Cabinet

The faint blue light above this aisle
recalls her first day in the hall
outside Pathology, her class in new whites
herded to a diamond of anticipation.
Now she hesitates before the vaults
of haddock, Cornish hens and rondelets.
In the mirror of the doors she sees herself
less clearly than the regiments of milks beyond.

In the shopping basket on her arm
a purse is crushed beneath four apples,
each illuminated as the face she contemplates
before this strange and public vanity.
When she waits before herself at home,
her eyes ascend the aphorisms
she has cut from magazines
Tomorrow is the first day...

Tonight her younger nurses bolted past her
as their shift was ending,
and she considered with an altered gravity:
I am ...I will be different.
She has dreams to take the place of dreams,
floating to her on this chill air of decision.

There is the dream in which she draws
a vial of hope into a cold syringe
and lays it on a linen, where it gleams.
Then the young nun tells her how
the chemo is a silver cobra frozen in its rage.
Outside the snow that melted on her windshield
has stiffened to a stubborn glaze.

FROM TWELVE CLEVELAND WINDOWS
(AFTER MARC CHAGALL)

A WINDOW FROM THE BRAHMS OPUS 51
*—for Lisa Boyko, Tanya Ell Woolfrey, Emma Shook
and Elayna Duitman*

Today the window of this barn opens to a
world within another, from the space above her
shoulder and her bow straining perfectly across
the open C's. There the clouds of dark birds rise and

swirl from the lines, amidst the spitting snows, urgent
in their ways as the souls of notes, just as difficult
to comprehend. Call it life or nature, as if
that were enough. The violins and cello joined

in her purpose to make a thing so deep and hard
emerge with just enough a struggle that it must
belong to every ear, those birds discovering
the frenzy that it is to live upon such strings.

ALL AT ONCE
—for Emma Shook and Eran Shiloh

He was searching for clouds, perhaps a star, when they
Appeared instead, as unexpected as a dream.
Walking to the little bridge, they seem tentative
As wrens at gloaming, fixed upon a summer moon.

He missed the moment when they stopped and leaned their bikes
Against the rail, just to gaze. Their heads move as if
Speaking. She leans enough to place her hand on top
Of his, a gesture like a rune of tenderness.

In such light the moon is pulsing like a heartbeat
As an aged man comes near, gentle as a mist,
His frosted beard a constellation, his fingers
Arcing as a wand to bless that sphere, those lovers.

COAL TRAIN: A WINDOW SOUTH

Encased in traffic on the Dina Dlugoz Bridge,
He can taste the fumes that he can see around him
As he did so long ago when the slag exploded
At the casting plant. Time, it seems, can go nowhere.

Below, from his window, a coal train frozen to
Its tracks, stretching all the way to West Virginia.
He is staring south, window to a memory.
The world's largest shovel there bottoming a strip.

In the maw of that bucket, his father and his
Best friend from the War stand beside a Chevrolet.
Was it door or exit, that pride of Hanna Coal?
Now he waits for something to move. But nothing does.

A WINDOW TO LIVES: THE ST. IGNATIUS ANNEX IN 1961.

First row, first seat. His vision on this slow morning
An accident of alphabet. The window from the
Old Annex. The city air in May already
Hot and filmy on his fingers and his notebook.

Through his window he can see another. One floor
Below, at the body shop next door a woman
In purple blouse and jeans has backed away from the
Grease-stained arms, but her right hand rests upon his belt.

She takes another step then suddenly turns again
And pulls him to her, their lips searching as they dance
Quickly from his sight. Caught by something new and strange.
Fifteen, and surging lives he cannot understand.

A Woman Buying Taffy Kisses

Perhaps only the wind
in the branches of the hidden elm
urged her from an iron bench beneath it.
None of that is in the photograph
by which she has become a figurine of grays—
babushka, dark raincoat, a gray hand
lugging a bulging shopping bag.
Her girth obscures the chalky panels
and glass of the booth in which
the clerk, a woman heavy in white
with a face like a walnut tufted
with black moss, trades a waxed bag
of kisses for a strip of tickets.
Where their hands meet they are as stiff
as Slavic grandmothers about to dance
with their sons. Where their hands meet
she holds a habit wrapped in paper,
and she clucks with her anxious tongue
its knowledge, its resinous amber.

Footprints: Three Songs for John Jackson (1950-2022)

"All journeys have secret destinations of which the traveler is unaware."

—Martin Buber

In Flight

In early April in 1983 you wanted photographs
Of Put-In-Bay for a calendar that never came to life.
Wind, whitecaps and rain were too rough for the ferry,
So we boarded the Ford Tri-Motor, Island Air,
We three friends the only passengers on that run
Searching the true meanings of restless in our souls.

Bouncing, swerving on the takeoff. The pilot turned
And shouted so we could hear, *"Don't worry folks. I seen
Much worse than this. Ain't lost no one yet!"* He snatched a rag
And reached outside to wipe oil from his window.
We learned how it felt to fly inside a Whirlpool on rinse.
The crosswind was so stiff he floated past the runway,

Landing on the wet grass, an act of faith
That nothing in our lives could comprehend.

At Frosty's

When a legend of a bar stands this empty, you can feel
The ghosts of everyone who ever walked within.
And stayed past closing, the ghosts of hope
We knew too well, the candled shimmer
Of lights seen through the line of fifths,
The lager held before us like a chalice.

But today we are the only three inside,
Chairs stacked upside down on empty tables.
We shook off the rain like puppies.
Our conspiracy that day was photographs,
As black and white and gray as the weather.

As we waited for the skies to clear, we shared
Stories long forgotten. Only the sharing remained.

TRACES

In the picture at the monument to peace,
I looked as fearful as I was, ducking from the wind.
So even the camera knew. And so did you.
We dreamed that there would be a calendar
With pictures and some poems, but some thoughts
Just evaporate. We let them go with a shrug or sigh.
Flying back in failing light, the noise and rattle
Didn't matter quite so much, the whitecaps beneath us
Churning towards Port Clinton. Still serious, you tried
To take a shot through the window, but neither
Planes nor lives would settle as we wished,
Not yet. You stayed my friend when I had few.

That last time when we looked at one another,
I knew why. The keeping on. The artist's fire.

A STORY ABOUT MOVING

Twelve, perhaps thirteen, she sits
at a counter in her new friend's house
carving the strawberries for dessert.
At first we lived in Muscatine,
and then we moved to Davenport.

This plainsong of her memory
suggests the meter of old utility poles
flashing through the blue glass of a dusk
beside the great, dark river. Moving again.
Her mother makes mistakes with men.

From every rent they dug their bulbs,
but here in Florida they can't abide the heat,
while she collects these stories
almost like gems to give in trade
for the very best of something still unknown.

Tomorrow they're moving to a house whose pool
is shadowed by tall oaks and oranges;
but, tonight, in her best friend's room,
the laughter comes and goes in showers
that will drown everything but dawn.

What the hell, I say.
It's late, and I'm hungry,
and this rain has got me
a little lost in Parkersburg.

So she turns
to take my order,
all freckles and a smile
behind the rotted screen.
Her purple t-shirt says
A Saint Ah Ain't,
her eyes the blue-black ice
of a deep mine.
"WudjawantAWNthem?

I tell myself, "You got to
stop this falling in love!"
But the late sun has broken
through the rain, which pools
in the ruts of the lot
into perfect red ponds.

Two Children Waiting for Their Mother

"Yes, I am stating that he and she were made from the
same clay, but born under different stars."
—Mary Jarrell

Outside the Recovery Center,
one child sits upon a concrete urn,
folding origami for her own tomorrows,
while her brother throws a tennis ball
against the curb. A little sigh escapes
before she asks if he can still describe
their father's face. "No, I can't remember
anymore." But the ball comes back
a little hard, bouncing off his hand and down
the parking lot. He just watches, as if
it were a stone he'd skipped across a pond.
His sister rises, stares into the window's clouds.
She leans to them, hands cupped about her eyes.

WHERE WE CAME IN

We always came in early, to see the ending first,
as if you understood instinctively
something about stories I should learn
by being there, plopped in fuzzy seats
right on the aisle. The figures on the screen
seemed awkward, disconnected from their voices
until we settled in, juggling the popcorn,
a sole pressed into sticky gum.

The Bridges at Toko-ri; William Holden,
his shot-up Panther falling in a heartless arc
that cannot reach the sea, and we wait
to see how he will live. Mickey Rooney
choppers in to save him, but they end up,
when their fighters leave,
scrambling in a yellow ditch to die
like rag dolls thrown against the muddy clay.

Within the picture others waited for the end
we already knew, saying things
that could not matter. Sometimes
it seems stranger than at others—
knowing how a story ends.
Watching you, I know we liked these men,
don't want them dying. I'm sure
that you'll explain a twist we missed.
It's *they* who have it wrong.

Dying was, for me, the simple "got you"
of a game. Embarrassing,
but you could live with it.

Count to ten and rise again. We counted
in the brush beneath the mammoth elms
and mapped our lives to come. But being dead,
we did have rules; we could not do anything
to let the world know we were there.

I watched the sunlight in the leaves.
Now I don't know what I made connections to,
drowsing through the glitzy Bank Night,
exaggerated smiles white as moons, walking
across the stage after their number's called.

Next time through I see it all
a wife, a child, Americans at play in Tokyo.
His lonely vigil in the ocean's spray,
his Panther lifting from the carrier.
We watch, entranced, the winding out
of someone's thread, an audience to destiny.
And still we think this time the shell will miss.
It doesn't and he dies again.

You don't say anything, and I leave sickened,
wanting something back, a whole Atomic Fireball
eroding in my stomach. I dragged a shoe
to lift a wedge of slush and caught
the cold half-moon as you picked me up.
I don't remember any words at all, one ride home
among a thousand, this one freighted
with the sour dread we'd left too soon.

That if we'd just watched long enough,
the little change he needed would occur.
For that portion of our lives it was
something that we did, a habit
that I'd like explained. I remember
only dimly other films, none so disturbing.
In my dreams he stumbles in the mustard of the clay,
this time with a glint of panic,
my eyes receding like a camera pulled away.

It's not a dream that I'm afraid of,
just a story from our lives,
a picture's flash of something real
I keep inside. But memories are different
launched with double ends. He dies, then
brings his family to Tokyo, embarrassed
naked in the common bath, laughing,

the dark carrier turning to the wind.

Carried to the parking lot, still tilted to the moon,
I know I counted ten for him, for us,
without illusion, until I fell asleep.
Last week I dreamed of something that we did,
riding the red scooter, me perched in front,
the sleeve of your t-shirt tickling my nose
almost to a sneeze, down Shaker by the Rapid
to your tractor, its radiator lying on a bank,
the tongues of solder almost white.

What were we doing there? You say
you don't remember, and yet I hold those
summer nights in Cleveland, endless, softer
than an elm with dew. Redwings and lazy gulls.
They're all just pieces. See how you've
infected me. I keep going back,
looking for the place where we came in,
afraid it could be anywhere.

Two years past on a job we shared,
I tried to call you from the trench.
Water lapping at your faithless knees,
the electric hammer laid across them
boring out the manhole's bricks,
red dust like smoke in wild plumes.
Lemme alone! I'm having fun!
Having watched and counted while the other lives
so often that the numbers take a place like stars.

I still see you evenings, as plain as water,
sitting under leaves that frame the faintest
constellation, a story where I'm there, not there
without a word of how our habits grew a reason,
as if a second later we'd have missed the chance,
            all our magic entrances.

A Laborer's Dreams

At the U.A.W. Softball Field

Where the little dozer droned
beneath a hazy, swollen sun,
pushing dust clouds back and forth until
they became this diamond lawn.

The copper plumes fall back upon their stacks,
a sort of weather.
These faces could be orchids
if orchids rooted in a foundry's soot
or bloomed as gray and bloodless
as this single race of ghosts
whose shift is ending.

Yet passed through showers
while vermilion stains their windshields,
they become again their different selves—
a laughing, teasing, jiving bazaar
of dancers in the muggy air.

They haul their coolers to the grass
they work with savage elegance,
like the throw so good it hits the runner.

From the other lot an engineer is watching,
leaning on the top of his convertible,
loosening his collar, staring vacantly.
Amid the pleading and the curses,
an arm is waving all the runners home.

And far above two crows are gliding,
keen upon the glint of something so familiar—
the utter heart of anger.

Open House at the Cleveland Valve Plant: 1996

*Fifty years he worked in that bitter factory. He learned
to love what I found so ugly.*

— James Wright

Walk the side streets where the honey locusts,
parched to yellowed parasols,
shade the tree lawns and the broken walks.

Here and there a sprinkler fizzes still,
arching from grass to driveway
in hope or stubbornness. Who can tell?

You might not believe that it could be so warm
in Ohio on this Sunday in October,
as furtive breezes snap the paper arrows
stapled to a sandwich board
past which the cars, like scarabs,
creep through the rusted gates
and squeeze the gravel of the lots.

In the languor of this day of rest
the old plant calls its children like a hymn.
And so the families assemble
from suburbs in the eastern hills,
from the weathered rows of GI homes
platted near the lake,
from Glenville, Euclid Beach, and Collinwood.

This sarcophagus of brick and glass and steel
coughs and trembles in the sun,
still by some miracle alive
amid the asphalt cracked and sealed
over the snakeskin blue and yellow clays,
behind the screens of dried-out shrubbery

Outside, a foreman and two stewards blink,
as if unaccustomed to this light
and lean across a table
handing bags of favors—a keychain
like a valve, some candy,
a U.A.W. thermometer.

So walk along the cedar planks
of the old factory floor
where the grease and creosote of decades
hold the shavings of a galaxy
whose history flickers in those lights
where anyone would notice him,
the pensioner whose crooked fingers
trace the stubble on his sunken cheek.
So obvious you'd think he was an actor.
And yet, the worn bandana blooming
from his trousers, the black oil in his pores,
the whispered words you cannot hear
and could never learn...

Is this old man like a scripture
or a dream? Who can tell?

You might not believe...
but never mind. Reach instead
across the exhibition ribbons
where new presses spill the valves
like nuggets into carts.
You could touch one,
let its ice bleed to your fingers
like a life, a made thing, after all.

CAUGHT ALIVE

He shuffles in the powdered clay,
like a boy raising his own brief storms.
Twenty-five feet of copper coiled on his shoulder,
Milky-yellow chalk staining the leather of his boots.
Trudging up the low slope under a white sun
As distant background, thin Doppler songs
of semis on an interstate hidden by trees.
The taste of dust, dust as pestilence.
One season fades to another, pieces of a whole life.

Here, he remembers the same unfinished road,
digging the water mains in winter,
clay trenched in ranges pocked with blue ice.
Delivered from black sleep, then,
to the late purple dawn, kerosene torches
melting the frozen tracks of the machines.
Diesels' coughing rattles. Cracking the frost line
of the soil, climbing into earth.

All day his hands are raked in their gloves
by the steel pipes, a slow, dark remembering
scaling the air, becoming ice. A man reaches
through a backhoe's arm to touch the same earth
like a wind, the wind of precipitous dreams
as sudden as voices to children:
Work a little longer. Things will change.

They change into slumber, into morning
where the light grows in inches
over the planet of mud, mud pulling
his muscles down, sucking his boots
into pools of the gashed earth.

Then it is spring, and the voice of waters
drips down the colored clays:
Too deep, too deep I love you.
He descends into the trench,

laboring the orange sewer pipes in place
It happened suddenly, as it almost always might.
Without a whisper of its own, the earth's grim passion
clasps him fractions from its perfect touch. No breath
but the quick meteors of force arched in his eyes,
the sky frozen in his eyes so that he thinks,
for a flash, *Why not be loved this way?*
Then thick arms pawing at his muddy clothes.
They needed him more.

Now he carries the copper of his summer.
He shifts the coil to the other shoulder to walk
along the ditch. This could be *his* dream, too.
He remembers how the dust came, and the redwings left.
Each night the seasons tumble to his sleep.
Today, though the world is dry, it is muddy in the hole.
They weave in pasty sweat, hooking up the bright fittings
through the hours. The other has the white, old belly,
the brutal soft hands, the eyes of a forest gone pale
with sun and years subtracted from dreams.
  Caught alive.

At LTV West

The last time a crow flew across this valley
it broke in pieces out of joy,
its yellow eyes the last to drift
to where you stood in the muddy lot
and watched the roofs recede like swells
upon a strange and vacant sea.

This old dragon is a dream of smoke and scales
that shivers up and down your spine.
Listen as the slag trucks groan and bounce
along the access road,
past the blackened drifts, the sumac,
grasses from the moons of Jupiter.
A flattened beach ball hangs unsalvaged
from a poplar's broken limb.

On this dream there's no agreement.
Remember or forget; it doesn't matter.
In this valley lensed with fire
only fly ash rises to escape,
while somewhere, in the weather of the furnace,
small beasts in silver stumble without gender
on the surface of the moon.

Stand in the red air, one side frozen,
one side burning. You, too,
can end the shift and corner in the oily light,
in your lap a plate of sausages and cabbage,
your tongue like pewter.

So dream your dream and choose a memory
while someone watching you
has seen a murderer's repose.

AT THE INDUSTRIAL ACCIDENTS CLINIC

As in Mozart's
Sinfonia Concertante
the movement into sour a pure
intent as an analysis of tear
reassembled to the sound I hear
in a page that is the same sour white
of lights you stood beneath.
We can take the skin
from the soft side of your thigh
and graft it to your finger.
So you told her to be accurate.
It didn't sound as long
as it would take,
your middle finger tapered
to a blade that I watch tremble
as a grass in wind. I figured
all along it was the earthquake
that shook you from the pallet,
put your hand into the rasping chain
like just anyone's. They called,
I came to find you gone back
to work already, so what is there
still to prove. We live, don't we?
Still, I come here to this place
with you where she sculpts
your old hand into something
at least good. While I'm waiting
in these padded seats they
must have stolen from Greyhound,
that chime is stuck, its call
a line of lemons just as the woman,
bent herself, pulls her husband
from the elevator.
He is coughing gray as April
when he hears it.
Where are we going? Where
are you taking me?

At the Amtrak Station: Elkhart, Indiana

Past the shuttered blocks of limestone,
past the weeping willows,
the train slows to the platform
where her solitary two-step
leaves her head a pace behind
the tinted windows of the cars.

She backs out of her eager dance
into a stillness nearly absolute,
lean in jeans and lemon halter,
her breasts contracted in a line
defining hope that waits on trains
for its fulfillment. *Again.*

Her hair is bright as black corn silk.
Behind her, at an angle, her cabby
naps inside a rusted Checker.

And two cars down a handler
lofts the baggage from his dolly
as she calculates the eyes of passengers.

The cigarette she doesn't smoke,
wedged between two fingers,
taps against her thigh the rhythm
of a rigid nonchalance, its *No*
suffused to purple in her eyes.

The Bleeder

He has done it again,
cheap gloves worn through,
his hands jellied by the tamper,
shop rags wound around them.

Barely, he can hold his shovel,
or navigate the traffic on 1A,
could touch without pain only,
he imagines, her face
the sun has tricked into his memory.

But this is his old story,
old beyond sorrow.
He will collect his pay,
finish out the week or just the day.

There will be others like it.
They will not last.

LEAVE

He walks awkwardly along the break wall
to get here where rocks stab out
into green Erie, he settles a distance
beyond the usual, sleepy fishermen.

Behind him the city is outstretched:
old granite, new steel, the red glass
of July's late sun, mirrored,
falling long across the emerald swells.

Small canyons split the hulks of stone.
The rock-gray rats scrape like paper
among the rubbish and dead fish, bloated,
washed to whiteness by the water's heights.

He perches on a slanted block,
his arms an ochre streaked with soil.
His hands open across his knees,
weigh the air and the light
the moment's waves deliver, weigh,
it seems, the flesh he has lived in,
torn, renewed, calloused with years.

Somewhere beyond those swells
is a body bent among shovels and pipes,
cursing, figuring a descent, an angle—
the incalculable years curled
into nights of one love's fingering
that this water carries from his sight
into its own deep dark.

A lone ore ship cuts the swollen star.
At the beach he left behind is a child
stooped to the soft foam and the evening,
watching the same ship plod beyond the sky
like memory. But he is here, now,
his eyes bathed in the water's sheen.

44

Going Home

Charles Day, aka
Sonny, yellow sport shirt,
jeans tucked in engineer boots,
gray sideburns. A man shaped
with old fence rails.

You cut a pump-jockey in Knoxville
and went the best way.
65 in a 40 in Ohio
and already a little high
on the "free air" of Detroit.
Passion is not clever.

"How old are you, Sonny?"
The judge is a moon
of spiny mucus—municipal court.
Leash laws and speeders!
"Sonny, they want you home."

So sag a little
in the August heat.
Sonny, you're older,
a deputy's holiday
through the tall corn and beans.
Piqua, Dayton—
all that openness shrinking back.
Corbin,
blue mountains.

SETBACK

Past winter dusk, a little drunk, he could not see
a chain across the drive of the abandoned station.
And now, like a tipsy Cossack dancing in slow motion,
he circles near and then retreats, two geysers steaming
from the hood of his Electra.

The driver's door ajar reveals, beneath the chalk-light
of the instruments, a railish leg of the woman
whose head pops out her window with a version of his name.
He punches at the steam, dipping leather of his overcoat into
the broken bourbon she has missed him with.
A streetlamp flares at him, leprous
on the windshield where it lines her face.

Flaying at the sky as if after strings he cannot see,
he wheels his foot against the fuming grille
in one pure anger. Even the air that hears
the fracture lets him fall with soft indifference as
she rushes to him, a glint of earring amber from the blinker.

County Roads

County Road No. 5

Wind rattles in the new barn.
It's all metal; the other burned.

A farm boy, fifteen, his body and age
No longer coalesce—he is already
Thick with labor, leaning forward
On the bales of hay
He has gathered for his sister's horse.

His frown recalls his dream,
Darker than the black ponds
Of his eyes.

I see the deer along the fence line,
caught in the drift,
but when I fire it changes
to my mother or my dad.
Everything slows down, and I watch
the bullet go in—and then
it is a deer again, stiff,
bleeding in the snow.

When I try to drag it in, I'm crying
and so tired. I never get it there.
and it changes again…they are so white.
I hear the wind and I always wake. Now,
I can't hunt without the dream.

His face opens with the waiting he has learned.
Farmers have the land and years, and
Effort is the patience not to understand,
for the world grows green with it.

Yet, there are no deer. He has never seen one.
They fight a lot. It's the noise I can't stand.
Leaving, he holds out hay to the horse.
The sky is November, Ohio slate—the fields

mustard and brown, raked clean by wind.
The gray deepens above the distant grove.
There will be snow.

County Road No. 6

He pulls the door to lock it.
On the milky glass he sees
his name in gold—
Florian H. Gearhart, D.D.S.

To be in gold the only dentist
in McCall, Ohio
has possibilities.
Farmwives bring their children
mostly these Saturdays
straight through high school.

The women come themselves
on weekdays, with complaint
to someone who is different
from the lean and tired shadows
in their homes until
he ceases to wonder.

He leaves his office
by the narrow stairs above
above the vacant Bolton Furniture
to his new, black Oldsmobile.

Main St., deserted for a while,
runs west to Leipsic
and east where he is going
to Findlay in the November afternoon.
Past Henke & Sons Building Supply,
its pyramids of tile fired orange
beside the piles of crushed limestone.
Further on, he passes, in a grove,
The tablets of his family
in the Methodist graveyard,
the grained light a haze around
the dark oaks, over the leafy grass.
Lengthened through his tinted glass,

is the life he has outlived
so many times—
hometown.
The acorns on the graves
still sting the lovers' autumn.
He remembers.

The wreaths are changed
each Friday until snow.
But no one here is different
long enough to matter,
the fields like ribbons of black marble.

He is thinking of Bermuda,
perhaps Mexico this year.
His soft fingers button the FM.
The Buckeyes are winning big.
Oh, Saturday.

Steak at the Sportsmen's Lounge.
What to say to the salad girl?

County Road No. 7

In November, after winter wheat,
An angel came to her in moonlight,
Stepping from a jade on the sill to her bed
Like a candle of linen. She must
Count the clouds each dawn,
Numbering the demons of her day
So that she wakes at three
And waits upon the enemies of the Lord.

At night the honey locusts in the yard
Are scarabs swaying in the air she hears
As song. All day she fears the pebbles in the drive
Might rise against her, so she walks far 'round
To feed the hens and talks of dangers
With Authority. Her husband is a vapor.

She calls him that, baking him
Angel food "to weaken him." His face
And hair aged to a mottled flint,
His whiskey thins him as she gains
What he subtracts in the equation of dominion.
When he stays later and later in the town,
She sees him anywhere she dreams.

This evening, she drives her daughters
To their rooms like geese, dresses as if
To go out, pins back her hair and plays
Upon her Wurlitzer the sacred Bach.
She sips her ice and grenadine.
Playing to the night with the fervor of her heavy flesh,
She sways, a blue reflection in the panes.
She will sanctify her house with the breath of hymns
Her angel will hear in three of his names.

He will come to her soon,
Touching the coals of her eyes.

A Migrant's Late Breakfast

"Want sum hep?" the hitcher says, and leans in bantering, while I tape the radiator hose. "That's gotter." He edges away, dipping green water from the culvert in a coffee cup and holding it out. "We can fill her this way." A face like one of those old skins the tribes laid out to dry. His lime sport shirt, at least a size too big, faded with sweat stains. Milky stubble, but eyes like two black flints. He smells a little bit like last night's wine.

He moved north from Florida with the pickers, a cousin somewhere near Fremont. Liked Ohio for tomatoes: "easy on the hands." The two of us in the shade of the pickup's hood, in clumsy silence, staring out across the sea of head-high corn.

"You're too young to hear of it, but I was at Chosin Reservoir." Got a hole in his gut "big as a silver dollar," and he peels up his shirt to show a scar as whorled as a tulip bulb. He can't eat so much since then but could take a breakfast. Implausibly frail, he shrinks into the corner of the cab as I nurse the truck towards town. I think he is singing something while he smokes.

There at the L&K I watch him dipping soggy toast into the eggs done easy, an arm held up for his refill. I fold the check between two fingers and start to slide, half-standing, out the booth. "That's good. I kin find my way from here."

A Summer Wife

Rained on last night, my marigolds,
sick with color and heat,
droop in their window box.
All around me
a morning's lingering disease—
the breakfast grease
still floating in the sink.
Cans and packages.
I can clean nothing

because it is too hot, because
this morning I just
don't want to move
from my chair, from the table
where the first flood of morning
has carried to formica—
cereal, paper, spilled sugar,
the burning fog of a man
who leans to the dull sun and is gone.

The strange sirens of houseflies
on the screens.
The ringing of humidity.

I want to say how even
my dreams of winter animals,
the wolves with eyes of red fire,
decay as the sick flowers.
One way of illusion.
My kitchen sauna,
my sinuses stoved with summer
as the final air,
betray all seasons.

The way my hands shrink
to January dryness
and my finger moves
in its cold ring.

Noon at the Wood County Fair: 1982

The cloudbanks loom like black mushrooms
far westward near Napoleon.
"Bless the farmers, curse the fair."

But here the pennants hang limp
in air sliced by the whirring rides,
near empty—a girl's scream seems half-hearted.

Along the rows of John Deeres, Fords,
and Allis-Chalmers the salesmen stand unbothered—
quiet and white as candles.

In the dusty midway mothers pull their children
past the booths whose hawkers chant like crows
a promise sour as a farmer's,

brittle as a husk. Even cotton candy,
losing interest, slumps in the heavy air.
In the parking lot a dog barks in sweet tercets.

Three men in overalls, skin as reddish ocher,
hang as vines upon the grandstand fence.
Their song of prices like a rasp,

struck silent as on the track a mule
has fallen at its sledge, its forelegs down,
its sudden gasp a whip across the air.

An Old Lineman Near the Wood County Home

He leans back in his harness, one arm
hooked idly on the topmost rung.
As the joke goes, he has lived here
nearly all his life. It is late August, after all,
and even the blackbirds cry for rain.

Through the years he has learned
to take the lineman's view of everything—
the crumbled cistern, white as chalk
amidst the drying corn. The asphalt
like a snake the crows pecked gray.

He sees a tractor's blue cough near Miñeta's barn.
Today the locusts buzz like relatives,
like the endless voices in the lines
crackling back and forth across this county.
Once, at noon, he was certain that he'd heard
his mother sobbing gently to the wind.
Once he had a wife with voices, too.

If he stares at the gray spiders on his arms,
if he thinks, just now, that nothing
is as long as this one life; if he remembers, at lunch,
some hornets crawling on golden pears…
But he tells no one what he sees.
It's too much like a story,
too much like an empty mirror.

Behind him and across the road
his rusted van rests in the drive
of the abandoned County Home.
The whispers of its bricks and cornices,
the ghostly faces in the panes,
are lost in canopies of beech and sycamore
as he watches the faint moon
and wonders out its silences.

BAD NUMBERS

On the way from work
I stopped the car to watch
some snowmobilers rage like bees
chancing everything on early ice.

I had been only checking messages,
still a thing so haunting strange…

Rodney, whoever you are,
the guard from Jackson
called to say
I guess you know
your brother passed away
last weekend.
He has some things here.

Somewhere, buried in those sentences,
lay an ember of kindness.
So I called and told him
the number's no good, too old.
The smell of wet wool everywhere.

When a child I watched
a grosbeak die against a window,
let it lie there dark as old blood,
let the darkness carry it away.

So now your brother's left you
some evidence to fold.
I hope they find you.
I hope some night
a whirl of dead leaves
scatters his name
into something you can love.

For the Town in Ohio Where No One Dreams

You tell me that your brother is content
to dwell in his town where no one dreams.

A lone catalpa, rooted in his yard,
has no stories whispered from its leaves,

which are as plain as bricks from Uhrichsville.
His son is clean as butcher's paper.

A town where no one dreams…no trains whistling
on the dew. The whole town smells like glue,

and sounds like a hymn no one wants to sing.
Did you catch the last dream out of town?

A dreamer these long years, I should cast blame.
But dreams are tricky. I knew a man

who dreamed a mall where only a meadow
had troubled his view. Tell your brother

you admire his resolve. It's not easy.
A bird's a spirit, a spirit is

a messenger hiding in our souls…
It can be too much. Last night's raven,

drooping with a candle in its talons
might be just a raven with a candle.

Ohio, I have loved you when I could.
But another old friend is dying.

Once I labored in the colored waters
of a sewer, and the rat that came

to hear the hammer stood up like a gnome.
Better to be a leaf that whispers.

Ohio, things are hard enough. Can you
forgive the dreamers and the dreamless

and just this once leave them alone?
You won't even have to love them.

THE WIDE PROSPECT

Looking the Other Way

I walked across what seemed the very edge of things,
above the ruins of the Sutro Baths
where the hills were cleared for restoration.
The stumps of cedar and eucalyptus,
carved as fresh as salad greens,
faced an ocean leaden as the sky,
as drear as any coast of Maine
that I had left behind…

I spent the morning walking the hills
at this hour, up Point Lobos, down Balboa,
every window in the city like a mirror.
In this city of obedient dogs two men
pause in a doorway, talking of the world.
A collie stares up listening.

Walking Ocean Beach, barely a wave to gurgle
on the sand and pebbles. A withered man
with a beard like moss lurched
toward me across the sand shouting
        "Rumsfeld! Rumsfeld! Rumsfeld!"

The land itself could not imagine this.
The Pacific was our first frontier.

Far out on the lolling waves
a warship knifes in silhouette.
its mast so unmistakable, gray on gray,
has caught a flare of sun hurled
from where I came. A sudden turn
to port and it shrank beyond horizon
to a vastness I had yet to comprehend.

GUEST WORKER

Age comes early to women
from Guangzhou. Her husband had
left in her the many ways

to become a foreigner.
She learned to sing, but will not,
like a dove who trusts no sun.

Ask her what she's doing here,
or not. That knowledge pierces
you too late to matter. Watch.

At dawn she works the patio,
bringing coffee, fruit and bagels
to golfers in drowsy haze.

In that moment she stands still,
flame trees caught in her black eyes,
newlyweds from Tokyo,

from Yokohama—leaning
to one another like vines—
wade into the gentle sea.

Song to the Moon at the Edge of the Philippine Sea

Moon in the dark heavens,
Your light shines far.
Your roam over the whole world
Gazing into human dwellings.
                    —from *Rusalka* by Antonin Dvorák
                              and Jaroslav Kvapil

All night the shadows flutter across the sand
as if stirred by something like a hand.
It is our same old moon but almost golden,
and its sheen a golden road across the sea,
through the lapping surf, the quiet pools and palms,
right to the balcony where I watch alone.

Yesterday, on the flight to Guam, Renèe Fleming
woke me with Rusalka's plea for love
that just might fall to anyone who stands alone
to watch the sky. Downstairs some tourists
from Japan do karaoke to "The Lovesick Blues"
in this place where it seems that I can walk
a beam right to the moon and turn and watch
all life below, including me upon that balcony
with the countenance of one who still believes.

And so in Chalan Kanoa, as if in a vision of the old,
two Chamorro cast their nets to the lagoon.
They murmur of a girl who swims forever
near the reef, her black hair streaming
under pewter heads of coral. Their wishes
float among the currents for centuries.
The lapping waves are drawn out like a sigh
that rides each tide across the world.
It sounded just as if they had an Eden
of their own, long lost among the names
of names of names…and when she surfaces
at last to breathe, her eyes like pearls,
she is alone. Those fishermen have slept
into a dream of acquisition—a jeep, a house,

a beer or three—just like anyone.
I am in Garapan, a stranger among those estranged.
The midnight sea whispers all its rumors:
The light, the dark, the old, the new intermingled
in a sadness that no human has redeemed.
What is demanded in the trade of States,
but lives, your lives. Your lives that might have been
have left upon the voyage that brought you here.

This moon will wane, its dust and rock
smoothed in its reflected light to something
worthy of a prayer. One hand, two hands
raised in air. If only words could span the distance
between us to human love when not even inches
bought with blood will matter here for long.
If it were only an ocean that rolled
its tides across our earth instead of those
we name as histories, would I still
stand here alone, longing in my soul
for that which disappoints, or disappears,
or never was…waiting as the Philippine Sea,
as warm as a breath, emerges as the world's
most perfect blue, as if it were an answer.

ON THE ROAD TO PALIKIR

Once he wrote that he held nothing
in his hands in happiness. Who else
could know how long I waited for you,
sleeping under stars I thought were fireflies
blinking in the leaves of black bamboo?
To wake alone in love requires
some illusion. *When your heart speaks, take
good notes.* I remember one hand
on the window, pressing your winter.

But here and now your voice plays in
my ear as if distance were the dream
while I climb this dark artery,
ramparts green in every hue one could
imagine. What can I show you passing
the wraith-like smoke of cooking fires,
a fleeting glimpse of bungalow,
old men squatting with sakau and betel nuts,
girls swaying in rain like purple fronds,
dogs like children, children like dogs
sitting in the puddles by the road?
In Kolonia my waitress
burst into a smile of pitted gold.
And I'm driving in a car with
no odometer to Palikir.

Why have you come here? Why? ask all
behind the orchids and hibiscus,
whispers like spiders in a cloud.
Mists float vines to webs of darkness,
ivory petals large as hands,
in their breath the scent of everything
that ever was alive. I stopped
and found a flower like your thigh
and waited for the wind to wash us
clear of distances forever.

BIKINI

It's out there, somewhere towards evening,
with small waves lapping at the coral sand.
So a stranger comes to Majuro and watches
as the clouds conform to an ageless dream.
He whispers that they seem "the breath of God,"
which is to say they might be anything.

If you listen, you can hear the trade winds
tell the story. God gave us this place
to be our home. It became the home of death.
This, too, is our history. First, we called it
Crossroads, then we called it Castle,
when the islands woke to a double sun.
Bikini, where we buried so many things:
Nagato, Saratoga, some goats, the lies
beneath the lies in the gray rehearsals
of the newsreels, the bland assurances.
And more than half the world's supply of film.
And the hundreds of Bikini
not a fraction in the scheme of things.

You would have thought by then
the world would know that with a God
you must have something in between—
a little wave, a nautilus, a storm,
some birds slanting above the currents.
But even here there was a brother like a wolf
who built his gift of ironwood to drown.

It's out there, somewhere towards evening,
the clouds swollen with the faces of removal:
Strauss, LeMay and Forrestal, these friends
of someone else's reasons. They said they needed
to drop the bomb to find out what would happen.
So go to Rongerik and starve. Go to Kili and starve.
Try living with the spirits of the dead.

It's out there, somewhere towards evening.
If you listen, you can hear the sailors
joking in the rain, hear the static in their bones.
Their stories beg forgiveness.
Try living with the spirits of the dead.
If you listen, you can hear the stars
in the breadfruit burning like tongues.
If you listen, you can hear the skins.
If you listen, you can hear the ticking years.

When can we all go home?
When we have waited long enough
to forget everything we knew.
There is a girl walking in flowered silk,
carrying a basket of fish with one arm,
hibiscus woven in her hair. She walks
beneath a line of palms with perfect shadows.
She is long dead now; she is still perfect,
even her shadow, even her smile.

A Child of a Soldier from the War
—for Hollie Ashworth

It was yesterday. Far at the end of Waikiki
a towel attendant stood in a tuxedo
in the shadow of a palm, near the chatter
of the bathers on the bright sand
crossed by pigeons white and orange and brown.
Listen, stranger, to the whispers of the waves.

What will happen if you say the words you cannot own?
Wai Momi, Ko'olau, Wai'anae. Will you see
the "river of pearls" beneath the warships' graves?
Will the mountains bring a rainbow
or a shadow that can pierce your heart for sixty years?

The driver of the shuttle tells a family of Koreans
how nearly every person coming to Hawai'i
goes to see the *Arizona,* a story
that dissolves within the silent avalanche
of rain and cloud that spills into the Ali Wai Canal.
So we listen to the stories, past the man
of middle age who has halted like a tourist,
staring, letting the water soak his skin.
Past the white dog sniffing the plumeria
blown onto the ground. Past the outcrop
of Tripler at Fort Shaffter, like a dried pink rose.

It's strange to think that memory has become
a kind of industry. But here in paradise
the world had changed or ended for so many…
who would and who would not be born
to stand and wait in the quiet lines
beneath the rain trees that hid nothing.
Hickam, Wheeler, Schofield, Pearl.
Here it seems that things are native only by degree.

Our parents are dying like days. At a table
three survivors of the *Arizona* sign mementos.
On the screens we watch their youth erupt
in flame and smoke and oil. They were children,
sporting under palms as if they owned the world.
For them the wars all started here, and so we ride
a launch in silence to a shroud above a tomb.

Read the books and gain perspective.
Count the names etched in the wall.
Watch the leis that drift across the tears.
Know someone who knows someone…
nothing helps you once you stand inside
and gaze across the harbor to the mountains.
Nothing helps you understand a world
about to learn death by the millions.

For so many years they were the mirrors
in which we could not see ourselves.
In New Guinea, one had watched the rain drip
from a skull propped like a chalice. One froze
his cheek against a cloud as the blossoms peeled a city.
One pulled a bloody penny from a tree in Belgium
and kept it with some pencils in a drawer.
One stood in lines for the entire war.

If they tried a million ways to mend
the lives they could believe in, then none
had explanations. Today the turret rusts above
the waters like a wound that will not heal.

In Puowaina you can find the grave
of Ernest Taylor Pyle laid between unknowns.
Once he told a story of running to his mother
from a serpent in the corn. Ride along the hills
above the houses painted in pastels. Watch below
the gray gulls turning like a hand to find the water.
Watch the flowers you can't name. Imagine,
for a while, that anyone came home.

Probably it is Time to Go

The beach at Kaimana is also known
as Sans Souci. Without, without, without...
The crumbling natatorium is closed.
An aging snorkeler will surface as
a dark seal, with a cirrus silvering his fur.
Paddlers stand their boards like masts.
Remember? I wanted to give you a place
where your lips stayed dark and moist into
eternity, where no heart could be shattered,
its dreams dispersed into this perfect blue.
One tall swimmer speaks German to the lifeguard,
who then bends to her breasts as if to better understand.
Another sits up on her towel and breathes,
her tattoos climbing like a zipper.
From Kapiolani Park, sagging men in spandex
slide beneath the neutered palms,
past me to the water where, as if to prove the terrible,
their phosphorescence guides the damned.
My purpose is to love you still, so who *are* you?
A jet is straining to escape, taking somewhere
people just like me, each one thinking,
"But they are not like me."

The Raft Boys of Majuro

Five boys use their hands and sticks
to maneuver an old door across
the lagoon, moving from one
outcrop of coral to another.
They never speak, just shift
and balance as if dancers
in some ballet they knew by heart.
And then, the sudden squall
in which two boys in front
grab the coral as if for life,
all ducking into the sheets of rain,
white t-shirts pulled like wet flags.

At the Ruins of Nan Madol

Even as the clansmen chew on betel nuts
and fold the dollars in a plastic bag,
the guide will struggle with the questions.
Micronesia is a summons to be heard once more.

Nan Madol stands as a reliquary of basalt
constructed in the mangrove waters where
these tourists traipse and gape and try to keep
their balance on the lumpy paths, brimmed
with passion to possess a world they never owned.
Bring nothing. Take nothing. Leave nothing.

These ruins once were someone's faith
that their now would last forever—
the *ketieu* to chase the ghosts away,
the women turned to stones or trees
for lack of tribute, the *pahi*
as a spell to calm the gods of war,
to appease the wind, the clouds, the waves.

These aliens will climb the darkened walls
in silence and gaze beyond the white spray at the reef
waiting for that blue expanse to whisper,
like the echo of a ghost, their mysteries.

In a Dream about Palau

Roosters crow and answer up and down
the sateen blackness of the hills,
and on this balcony of the 7 Stars at 4:00 AM
I hold my coffee with both hands.
At some distance there is one whose call
lasts longer than the others, if only by a second.
Those voices cover one another like a round.

If you were in Kolonia, you would
have waked me from a dream about Palau,
where a witch rose from the mangrove
and sang a promise that each stranger to Koror
would find enchantment never seen before.
The legends say a British tar went crazy there,
murmuring his wishes to the rattling fronds,
gone missing in a pistil of hibiscus.
Yet Palau is just an island, a story,
a dream. We have never been there.
I hold you in both hands, feeling your heartbeat,
drifting in your eyes, knowing
there was a scent of syrup, a tongue
of the darker always from which you take me,
your lips more real than any other bloom
of such desire and, unlike paradise,
tasted best without illusion.

1870, A Missionary Dreams Perhaps of Poetry

In Mesenieng[1], this holy place, his dreams
Drift upon the trades like seeds.

It started with a vision of a girl,
Her legs a shade of caramel,
Walking down a path beside a swimming pond,
The rust soil shaded by a stand of ironwoods
Aligned by colonists to remind themselves
Of their own geometries, or perhaps
To offer the souls of Kolonie a glimpse
Of what could lie beyond…if only they believe.

And yet, all night she walked his dreams,
Turning back to smile. So, he woke early
On his already steaming morning,
Sitting on the stone steps of his chapel,
Both hands on the cup of tea he will not drink.

Across the path from what's become a town
He sees three girls in yellow wraps,
Reaching with the languor of a dance,
Gathering the breadfruit into baskets.

He sees each girl has wound
Hibiscus in her midnight hair.
He whispers as if quoting an epistle:
"If only they believe as I believe…"
And sets the cup between his knees.

He remembers the moment he arrived,
Walking down the pier of rocks
And staring at the mountains,
Their deep green smoking in the mist,
The perfume of their orchids

---

1 Mesenieng was the traditional name for the sacred area within the current
port town of Kolonia in Pohnpei, FSM. It translates as "Face of the wind."

Promising the possibility,
The specter at last of what was lost.

As he woke his feet and hands
Still felt the snows of Concord.
Once upon a time,
All his dreams were filled with snows
And the pure, cold path to paradise.

He anticipates the Sabbath
To count the souls that he has saved.
And yet each night he counts instead
That girl who walks among his dreams,
Turning with that smile until he wakes
And mutters to the torpid air
"Oh Lord, what is this place"?

He is old enough to wonder,
"Should I doubt my faith
Or doubt my dreams."

So he waits, and waits another day
For the voice of God to answer.

Rainsong of a Feral Dog in Palikir

I cannot know what she is thinking, but, with
Her eight teats stretched almost dragging on the road,
I can see she has a mother's eye for traffic,
Stopping even as the back door of a cab
Swings open suddenly, so that the stream
Of spittle brewed from betel nut will find nothing
But a puddle in the asphalt.

It is, of course, a paradox. The timeless and the quick
Both live together here. I could almost quite believe
The world began as quickly as the stories say.
A rain, some sun, and suddenly a world appeared.
And death as quick as well. Maybe that is why
The flowers and the trees here seem so brilliant.
Nothing can waste a breath awaiting blooms.

So, she will cross the road in rain
And lie beside the shoulder, as if she seems
To understand the edge of every danger.
But who can say such things with certainty?
Even wisdom can miscalculate
No matter how its earned.
The next curve makes her disappear.
More dogs, more rain, more children walking
Off to school in purple jumpers
As if there were no rain at all.

But as I wait my turn to pass the bridge
I am thinking of her still, stretched out
yellow in the ruddy mud, waiting, waiting.
Where to be alive is just enough.

Living Beneath the Shades

Here the tourists say with endless ease,
Well, if you must be homeless…

But when the world becomes so simple,
The truly wise will stumble on a caution.
In any life, the chances to do one thing
Or another will multiply like ghosts
Who speak in parables instead of dreams.
They flood the mind and flood the soul.

Watch the strange doves walking
In the parks beneath the neutered palms,
Beside the ironwoods, the monkey pods,
A paradise with maintenance.
Stand beside the banyans, brought here
Long ago to stand like houses.

Some boys are braving the tropic sun,
Playing soccer in Kapiolani Park.
In the history of this ocean
Hawai'i has always held the center stage
In the cold desires of nations.
Yes, there is much to see beneath the shades

In plastic bags from ABC, they haul
From next to next their store of choices,
Some they make their own; some made
By strangers come to change this place forever.

These wanderers are curious,
Or inconvenient. At dawn they quiver
Underneath a cone of tarps
Or mounds of dirty towels.
On Kanekapolei, near what used
To be King's Village, a haggard woman
Rises from the walk and says to no one
"My name is Irene. What's yours?

What's yours? I said my name's Irene!
What is wrong with you?"
She is shaking with the menace of the lost.
A life stripped down to this...
It could frighten anyone; the just, the kind,
The mocking can all be solved to equal here.

Along the Ala Wai Canal a man
Whose age is just impossible to know
Sleeps upon a bench beside a grocery cart
Topped with wares inadequate for explanation.
A blossom of plumeria has fallen
On his shin, and twitching at a snore,
Is lofted like a butterfly.

In the Belly of Ala Moana

In this new Hawai'i, in this someone's dream
Of perfect dragons sleeping on their gold,
In the lights that gleam like magma,
As if they truly do belong, truly do
Illuminate the circles of a world
You enter without fear or caution.
It matters little what you thought
You wanted when you chose
To brave this lair. The choice of what
You should desire has been made.

Everything is just the latest trend.
Everything beckons with a woman's hand,
And she, of course, is perfect, too.
Past the kiosks and the stalls,
Past the windows where you see yourself
In what they sell, past the shoppers
In hypnotic trance of joy.

Your memories, Hawai'i as it was, are lost
Among the legacies of broken kings,
Of queens long dispossessed.
The *path to the sea* has been cleansed.
A way out of this place is now
The only thing you cannot buy.

CANTARE TO THE HAUNTS OF POWER

In the Matter of A.M. Galinova

1. Alexandra Marisovna Galinova (1943-1970)

She was not, at first, obedient to history.
Once she said to me, "Why do you ask me this
when you already have an answer?"
With her, you could not just put down your cup
and sigh, as if the questions had been
merely philosophical although,
as technique, that was among my best.
This same photograph was on my desk—
a butterfly hanging above three dark tulips,
a gift from a lover addicted to irony.
It is better to simply know and then forget,
to sleep in peace without a dream.

But somehow I've outlasted my vocation.
When the leaves have fallen and curled
in the usual way like brown, dead hands,
I am a man with voices stretched and dried inside.
At the end, do we become the same book after all?

It is well enough that the graves are lost.
And yet, I recall Galinova above the rest.
She had the most talkative eyes,
for which I am the only evidence.
It would have been better for me, I fear,
that she had never breathed one cup of air.

2. Galinova's Only Recorded Dream

According to the record, it took fifteen days
for Galinova to share her dream with me completely.

Of course, I began by simply looking around.
I had awakened sitting in a room
with coarsely painted red walls,
and then five silent old men

in brown tunics, propped upon a bench
against the wall. I knew that each
was a different enemy of my soul,
but they neither spoke nor moved.

Then a more familiar man entered the room.
He had the mustache of an old willow,
and I understood at once
that he was more clever than most.
He walked directly to me
with such an even pace, and I noticed
the sprig of white hair in his ears
and the small white box in his hands like a gift.
He bowed slightly; then he took my hands
and began to remove my fingers,
laying each in the box like cigarettes.
Then he reached up and with a flick
of his fingers popped out each eyeball
and softly placed them beside the fingers.
Then, using both hands, he removed my tongue.

At last he spoke, saying he needed
but one more thing — the name
of that which I loved most.
But how was I to answer?

He smiled, a half-smile, really, closed the box
and left. Then it began to rain,
a not unpleasant warm rain.
So ended her telling of the dream,
which I kept the way a priest accepts a soul.
But for a few days after, I received
only the most perfunctory answers.

3. Her Interrogator Considers the File

Tonight there is a wind of something scratching,
like a squirrel in the ice along the eaves.
I spread her pages on the table,
all the vowels like little black coins.

Through years of trying I have learned
that it's best to let the memory die slowly,
to make barren, finally, even the soil of things
unspoken. But with Galinova, there's some uncertainty,
some risk that, at the end, she was simply mad.
She said that words were killing themselves
inside her head, like bees flying against a wall.

Then it was after some days, perhaps a week—here
the file is not precise—that she began to lose
the names of cousins, and quickly after that
her friends and lovers disappeared
almost in bundles. It was rewarding to observe
how many she had seemed to lose all by herself.
But we found *every* name she knew.
It is like the light leaving when a door closes
until there is a room completely empty.

A room completely empty.
I was pleased with that.
It became the motto of our group.
You could see it painted on the door.
My old boss was laughing. "Be careful.
Poets are not needed here."

That Galinova. When she sang of gourds,
white gourds smiling in the web of poplars,
I almost smiled. When they are free,
they can't remember even angels.
But Galinova, near the end,
her songs were just too crazy,
just a little bit beyond my reach.

The trick is to be patient.
I made her love me.
I made her tell me everything.
The trick is to know the proper balances.
Those who say it's just a matter of technique
are simply amateurs of pain and cold
and light and waking,
of the last, ingratiating smile.

I know she's dead.
I know that, just like the others,
she took the bullet with a smile.
And yet my secret lingers like a cough.
I think I might have botched the job.
Alexandra Marisovna Galinova,
tell me there is nothing left but paper.
When I look at these old pages,
it's as if I am surrounded by something,
by someone, ingeniously dead.
Her eyes that last time…
like the eyes of a seal still
wishing to give me something else.

In our profession there's a saying.
There is a house with a number you can't walk past.
It is a house without windows, without doors.
And it is not silent.

When you see it, when you hear it,
then you know that you have lived there
as good as all your life; and you will never
leave it again, not even in a dream.

TULAGI

Where it happens. Kneeling
with such slowness he pours
the hot sand into his bloody palm,
as if he were counting something
saved for this moment, perhaps
the thoughts he cannot hold
over a small but painful wound.
His fingers splayed like compass needles
to each point where the world goes on.
The sun navigates his veins
and he cannot hear himself.

Because of him something has happened.
His grandson rinses suds from the hubcap
for the first time, and wants to be alone
bearing the cold of the spray, watching
the water on the sun of the chrome.

Does he lie or not to the boy, saying
"It was so long ago I don't remember
much." He tells him absently
of a dawn when the sea seemed brown
beneath the pink sky someone should paint.

He wanders to the curb to get
his empty rubbish can, following
the cold stream down the asphalt,
catching his heel in the soft, hot
tar of the sealer. It is a noise
that churns in him, the false step
to small accident.

Gazing at his green lawn,
at his neighbor's lawns as stupid
and relentless ironies, he whispers
all in threes like pills: "It had to be ...
It had to be ... It had to be."

Still, he is uneasy, for
the boy, listening, is like a hole
in which the facts fall out of sight.

The forty-year-old fact he gave him
about the polar bear, how fast it runs
compared to a man, he took
from the dying corporal in a rotting tent
because the tent looked like an arctic sky,
because the bear's cold, final rage
meant nothing to the bear, alone.

Later, with the rain near,
he sleeps strangely, as a man who
has stolen something, undetected,
and forgotten what it was, or
whether it was worth it.

When at last he dreams,
he kneels with red snow in his hand
over the carcass of the white bear.
His mouth is open, slack, as if
there were a wind to take his words;
and his eyes, like black plums,
stare helplessly out to himself
who is watching.

To J. Robert Oppenheimer, September. 4, 1983

I took my usual walk this evening
across the clover field to the river,
where I startled three ducks into an ellipse
of flight over the dull water,
but I still had your radio voice in my ears.

This is the anniversary of a day's worth of things
for a long time, among them me.
And I had your voice in my ears
as a breeze while the ducks
were lost beyond the still green birches.
"I am become death, the destroyer of worlds."
And later, "I don't know. I'm not
close enough to the facts now."

There was an innuendo that you
were a vain man and could be cruel
to those who loved you. Here,
the asters have begun to die,
a slow decay almost felt before it's seen.

It's natural to want someone to blame.
There were others who loved
that thunderous speech of stars, who
spoke it like a Christian learning Greek.
A human will love anything, it's true.

Back beyond the fields,
across the sky is Ohio.
I have loved many strange things myself
in this life you knew something of before
I ever could. I don't blame you. You suffered.
But I'm curious. When did you understand?

I have loved many strange things
myself. I wish you could hear tonight
the cicadas waking in this field like citizens.

You could, if you weren't so dead,
walk among them in your porkpie hat.
You could be in love.

No one would listen.
No one would ever know.

Eight Lost Photos by Andre Kertèsz

A Soldier's Allegory of Memory: 1918

It lacks some clarity. It is a little crude.
We see him only from behind as he tries
to grow smaller in the world that wants him dead.
It is so ordinary, the dirty overcoat pulled
about him like a blanket, the long collar
turned up, the dark mushroom of a *Pickelhaube*.
We cannot tell what he might see if one thing
were truly like another, as in a story he remembered,
for now, to him, all memories are casualties.
The gray mound in the distance shows some rocks,
something like a canister, something in a foot of sleeve.

If only once his father brought him to a glade
and left him while he cut a tree...
If there had been a lake of dead stars
like ashes in oil, if blood were like rain.

Edward Teller in Munich: 1929

No one knows this student at his coffee.
He frames the guarded posture of a refugee,
this Jew who fled to Germany. He has three books
laid open on the table, but he does not read,
not even the letter he holds with both hands
like a scripture. His cup breathes like a mist
upon a mirror. The Vanilla Revolution
left him darker, the streetcar cut his foot away,
and a shadow bleeds beneath his brows.
He is, perhaps, as incidental as a bird.
His black eyes find the sun beyond the linden,
Like someone who is waiting to believe.

A Cellist and His Lover, Asleep: 1935

Why would we care that he is nearly naked
in a chair, mouth open, a towel and bow
across his sagging thighs, his breast as clean
as silver? His wish had been to be different.
In bed she is tangled in a snow of covers,
so that only her hair is seen, a shock
of black wheat. Three black shoes adorn a pillow.
On a pile of books two candles light a dragon's eyes.

You could tell him art should never be so cruel.
He had tried the Bloch, but his arms proved just
too short for his desire. For him, the century
had nowhere left to go…after all of this,
the absence of surprise. But on the mantle
her parakeet is pecking at its mirror.

A Portrait of Ordinary Desire: Normandy, 1939

You would need to stand upon a ledge to see them
nearly hidden in the sand between the rocks.
They embrace as if waltzing sitting down.
Their beach clothes sag upon them as if stolen,
with wide stripes like a candy. The wind from sea
has lifted her white cloud of hair, while his seems oiled
as a seal's. White roses lie askew across a hamper.
From this height you cannot discern their eyes, but
his hand pulls hard enough to bend her shoulder.
Her gaze drifts past him, to gulls upon a swell.

The Light of Heaven in Glass: 1945

At first the shaft of light is dancing
like the chatter of an angel pitched
beyond a human ear forever.
But something lives in that buckled cube
that was a window, then a lantern,
then a chalice, then a mirror.

Or it is nothing, a light without
a shadow, not even the child of sand.
For in heaven, only one who looks
is human. Who else would have wondered?

A Russian Engineer at Tea: 1953

She had merely leaned back from the table,
her left hand pulling the dark shawl closer
in the breeze that lifts her sheaf of calculations,
to which she has added nothing for an hour.
The gray wolves of those numbers, like her eyes,
have trailed some perfection into shadows.
A Russian has too many words for sorrow.
Still, that clear face might have been some angel's.

But her slide rule is propped against a saucer
that barely holds the shadow of an alder.
But her orphaned cup of tea has blackened
like a memory, like her mother's blood,
down the stones beneath a drunken lover's door.
Therefore, now she has a smile without a smile
at the white moth settled on her pencil.
The word is almost nesting on her soul.

The Tractor and the Boy: 1962

We desire this portrait of someone
who belongs. His shoulder leans against
the tire as if it were a mule
that he has known for both their lives.
Someone has coaxed his smile, his hair
is a crop grown wild past its season,
his black eyes like ravens. Behind him such
perfection. A gray cat tears its mouse in straw.
The tractor lifts a stream of silver
to the silver sky. The soybeans restless
as a sea, the dark welcome of the poplars.

A Street in the New World: 1970

Is it as gray as a lizard's tongue, this street
without even a human shadow?
It unfolds from the perspective of a wind,
past the fires of broken glass, past
a dark hulk of Buick with its eyes gouged out,
the pastes of newsprint on a fence,
beyond the boarded windows of a school whose
painted lessons linger: *Shit on it all! ROM!*
Fuck a planet today! We must
forget this street because we are moving on.
It is always noon here. Nothing
remains but the terms for what we do not need.

When a Poet Begins to Wonder about Love
—for Petr Mikeš

When the poet begins to wonder about love,
perhaps there will be solace in memory.

There, you see, the bare lamp swayed
in drafts from the broken sill.

There the freight elevator groaned slowly to your floor.
The grate shone where a thumb slipped in the grease.

Perhaps someone came to question you, searching
for the evidence of words locked into poems.

Oh, about love. She is elsewhere. Don't even
our enemies have our best interests at heart.

But now is not then, and we decided
long ago that memory is not for comfort.

So how is the small stone house in which
you live freely? How is the undisturbed night?

How is the machine that prints words
faster than they can be written?

Here the melting snow pools in a brown meadow.
So let us wonder about love.

A Scene from a War

The young Italian, a soldier,
has found love
in an August of the *guerra*.
He flees the shattered town
in the Ukraine, seeking his lover,
who is running ahead of his sight.

She has become the white flame
of the star that has stood still
in the sky of his hopeless war.
She has seen this earth by her own
lights and flees with terrible speed
as the armies turn like weather.

He feels the shadow of a single cloud.
For a moment, he is surprised
that he cannot run, as in a dream,
and bees have cut the sunflowers
down in anger, with the black soil
smeared like paste upon his sleeves.

Neither of them had spoken
one word the other knows.

A Colonel in Waikiki

He says the name by his medallion
Means nothing to him now.
In the front seat there's a half-eaten
Bowl of rice, chopsticks tumbled
To the floor, a jumbo Dunkin' Donuts mug
Jammed into the holder, some papers
In a language I can't understand.

In Viet Nam I had a regiment.
Here I have this cab. I can never
Go home. They would kill me…
The Communists! The Communists!

Not knowing what to say, I remind him
Of the number. *I know every street*
In Honolulu. Thirty-two years!
Yet he stares through the window
As if driving blind. We are both
A little lost it seems, searching for
Our better. His is distant, somewhere
In the mountains, in the cooling mist
after monsoon. Mine beside a moon
I cannot see. I surrender. I do not
Ask what he would never tell.
Take me back. Maybe I will find
A home I can remember.

KOLONIA: BREAKFAST WITH SOFT CHATTER OF THE HUMANS FROM THE NGOs

While waiting for their coffee or their tea,
They tilt their tablets so they all can see
The slides they will present to this Minister
Or that one, or maybe to the Under-Secretary.

Their postures do reveal the ease of those
Who know in full just how the World should be.
Their accents spill together softly, like rivulets
That join to make a stream. In a story older
Than this *place above the altar*, the white hibiscus
Swallowing a pillar just below bears them all in silence.

One is even stunning in this light, a jewel
Underneath a curl around her ear.
Her calf that flexes through the rayon…
One is left to wonder whose world is this
As the fees are wired everywhere but here.

The clouds, as always, building in the east upon
The winds of trade and pass into tomorrow.

After the Death of Paul Tibbets in 1992

It is the flight of August in Ohio.
Cicadas trill the very hours of the day
and never think of how they'll be remembered.
They die as all things do we cannot see.
It doesn't matter. If *you* are remembered,
it will always be on someone else's terms.

Your passion was to fly beyond it all.
You were among the best at something savage,
which is to say that you became a moment
in a calculation, one in which the blossoms
of Nippon did not have to fall to die,
but merely walk about their days.
Perhaps it's true that you saved
more lives than those you took away,
an explanation added to the file.

From that frozen altitude you waited,
the blinking lights empaneled in a doom,
the release a sudden breath above those angels.
You bent a wing to safety, left gazing
at your deed "still boiling like something
terribly alive." A precious word, alive.

If only irony were truly an awakening,
a place to stand among the clouds of reasons.
You lasted long enough for *this*?
Some might welcome as a judgment
that you dared not even mark your grave.
Your voice is lost and leaden as a page.
Yet it is summer in Ohio.
         We might still hear anything.

Leaving Hungnam: December 24, 1950

You survived the road from Yudam-ni,
and you are leaving with your fury,
your sorrow and your dead, and
with all you can retrieve.

From out to sea you watch
The black blossoms walk along
The buildings and the piers.
Everything remains a danger.
But there is always a story
no one sees; a boy scurries
in this trigonometry of death
like a squirrel seeking morsels
wherever they might be found,
his life or death reduced to fantasy.

Such destruction is a habit
that's been honed through practice.
Stand off now. Be at peace.
Try sailing to Pusan, and,
for a moment, find your star.
It is not your world that ends today.

TALES FROM AWAY

THE DREAM OF THE LAST LOON

Long past midnight, carrying through
My screens, it cries for its mate.
I hear with it the answer of silence.
It calls again, and again.
I wonder what it has learned
Of desire and loss, this ancient
Bird that wishes only to be safe
In love from hunger.
A prayer is also a lament,
It seems. It cries once more,
And I can see the red moon
In its eye as it floats beside the reeds.
The echo of nothing, drifting.

An Explanation of Butterflies

It was like any struggle with memory.
She walked beside a stand of tamaracks,
almost lime in their freshness,
when first a black, then a yellow butterfly
danced so drunkenly beneath the limbs
too slowly to vanish as they did.

It was not the first time
she had swallowed her own breath.
Once upon a time, some fireflies
were clumped like dirty salt
in a jar on her bedstand beside
a Monarch glued to cardboard with a name.

But her walk was yesterday.
She holds her teacup like a black crystal
in which she cannot quite believe.
When they came, she had bent listening
merely for her name among the asters,
as if they were a world that might remember.

In Its Season

It is nearly true winter, but only enough
snow to cover some of the headstones
over which the mourners troop, trying
to keep their balance on the pillowed ground,
in the shifting wind, so that we might
have tears just standing here even
without this young death we feel as
a weather from which there is no indoors.

The spray of pine and cones upon the casket,
like a wreath upon a door to call us
into a season counting its birth of hope.
If she lit her hope to candles, they are
as distant now as stars, as cold
as stars seem. It is wrong.
Being human we want a thing to blame.

So let us blame the sky. Looking back
from this graveyard, along the valley
of the Carrabassett, we see it too is wrong,
racing blue and copper as a thunderstorm
August in its danger. In its season

the storm never quite in us breaks.
We gather and disperse, crunching and
sliding to our cars, wordless in early night.

Later, when the sky has begun to clear,
when snow has drifted to the fresh earth,
in her deep, blue forest beyond her grave,
a doe has stood from its needles
and turned its ear to the wind.

Through the boughs, frozen in a dark eye,
the light of one star made near.

In a Parking Lot at Rockland Harbor

The perfect sunlight is an accident.
You might see him any day at noon.
An old lobsterman, a new Ford.
He needs little from his eyes to follow
as you walk beside, and then behind.
His face like a brown, stained bag
from decades in the open air he leans to still,
his chin almost at rest upon the steering wheel,
a purpled ear precisely sealed against
some ailment by cotton, gauze, and tape.

It is mid-day; it is summer,
and pleasure craft traverse the harbor.
A dozen guillemots bob like blossoms
beneath the ceaseless cackles of gulls.
What dances in that pure light gathered
in his lenses as his dark hands pull upon the wheel:
the diamond chop, the islands, a life
as singular as granite broken free?

His denim shirt is buttoned at the collar.
And though the wind blows hard offshore,
in his mind, perhaps, he feels its shift—
a sudden whip of spray, a subtle loss
of balance in the swells beyond Matinicus.

One finger slides to tap the dash,
and his mouth moves like a turtle's,
chanting something to himself, to himself alone.

Here, There and Away

In the basement of this funeral home there is a room whose walls are lined with school pictures, pictures of children gazing hopefully, or slightly goofy, from the fading gray and chalk of paper printed for the generation leaving now. Sometimes it is easy to imagine that an old enough world had no color until granted it by film.

Outside the rain we hoped would wait is falling, drenching Cleveland, bleaching the October leaves, bending them with a sting of northern air. The day unfolding, its sky so darkly mortal, swamps the cheer of modern liturgy in the Mass of Christian Burial. Six soaked pallbearers struggle with their oak burden on slick grass, to a white tent sagging above an envelope of earth. *Put your rose upon the casket as you leave.*

I emerge into the rain, part of a blur of mourners, to realize that I am home once more. Cleveland. Driving from the neighborhood where I was born to the one where I grew up carries me along the lake, across the heart of this city, less freighted than it used to be with the smoke and fires of mills and factories—industry as climate. The river thinned of the long ships that emptied out the hills of taconite. The old granite, the glass and steel of renewal, the lake—especially the lake—are gray as any Cleveland joke. But it's all right. More than that, amazing. Amazing to see something for, could it be, the thousandth time and know that it is different. The angle of light changed so slightly upon a wave that spends its energy a second earlier. The lake gulls riding a different wind.

Far out on the breakwall a fisherman has climbed a block above his usual perch and pulled his collar tighter. Than when? Than ever before, or perhaps, again. It doesn't matter, for the place is in the moment, and that is where the artist lives. In the place in the moment. It's all right, this Cleveland.

Martin Luther King Drive was once called Liberty Boulevard. It winds through the gardens of the nationalities, as fixed in another era as those pale photographs, to the Cleveland Museum of Art. To Winslow Homer. To Maine.

Have you ever stumbled into something that exploded with surprise? When every receptor in your heart and mind and soul and circumstance was set only to receive the very thing, just out of sight, you never figured on? So it has been, for this flatlander, with Maine. With Ohio. With Cleveland, with some few humans. Rooms with doors to other rooms. And so, with *Reckoning with Winslow Homer*.

᪤᪤᪤᪤᪤᪤᪤᪤᪤

The first time I stood upon the coast of Maine it was as I imagined it, which was not what I expected. A poet's early lesson in surprise. I had feared that my imagination would be wrong, that the place could not match the mythic image it held for me—a mix of photographic seeds, Great Lakes reckonings, wistful rumors, undergraduate permutations of *Dover Beach*.

It must have been somewhere near Camden Hills. I remember the mix of salt air and pine. Now I'm glad my first visit was not to a mud flat at low tide. The shore lay as rough as an aftermath of battle, rocks that seemed so permanent in contrast to the sandy beaches of my childhood. The sheer, almost boundless power of the sea as even small waves broke with stunning violence. But most of all, and still, the chill sense of the northern ocean, the very cusp of the end of the world, fish as sudden as razors.

I turned my back to the land to gauge the thunder of the waves. In Ohio I would watch my father stand outside and stare into the wildness of a Midwest thunderstorm sweeping off the lake. I stood six feet less brave, my face pressing the storm door's screen, my eyes as frozen to the danger as to that heart's yearning that each of us casts out, trying to net some fragment of a life beyond us. Slivers of a mirror in some moment the lightning found. The pure force of particulars in the moment, in the place where someone stands alone, wishing not to be alone.

Imagine a necklace of lightning, strung together bolt by bolt. A necklace of the froths of waves, their curve, the color of their

112

lights. To make these someone stands both in and out of the moment, anchored with a soft ferocity. For the maker, it is exactly that original apprehension only once. Then it is a gift that others see from where they stand in moments further out. The fragments of the story are brushed into a sadness fixed and final.

The painting, as does the poem, becomes the thing we never snare entirely. And that fact we learn to love. Waiting, watching, summoning the sums of our particular lives like lenses. A story.

Beyond his primal vision, or as part of it, I see that Winslow Homer paints a story in everything he does. And the stories accumulate their moments to the moment that he tells and point a way beyond the canvas to... *Moonlight on the Water*, where the night wave, as it reaches land, has cast upon it the bursting waters of the moon. And looking down we see the two who watch are small and dark, in a cloth of midnight as surely formed as any granite. To watch someone watching is a story. And this story, enlarged, becomes the different story of *A Summer Night*. Sometimes it is possible to imagine each of us as a study for another's canvas. And then the two for yet another...

☙☙☙☙☙☙☙☙☙

I think I went to the Museum that day because to do so felt just like the story I was living in. To my disgrace, I had thought of Winslow Homer as a figure from a dim past who painted postcard scenes. In the cavern of the gallery the viewers drifted in random paths, clustering before a work, then passing through each other.

At the first canvas I was gone. The storms stark and powerful; each drew me. I couldn't even read the titles. Here I was a half a century before my birth in a moment that I knew. I stayed until the angles of the land and wave and sky, their colors, had metamorphosed into their separate works. Until I truly told the difference.

A mortal day of loss forms such a conscious day. To make art is, in part, to understand the difference between the things from which we go and those we can't leave anywhere. Someone reading souls could find our true hieroglyphics in the moment of that knowledge. Maine, Ohio, Homer, Cleveland, the stories carried in my veins, the images of a sad hopefulness, are all illuminated here.

There is a story, apocryphal perhaps, about Winslow Homer waiting six weeks for a wave to break the way he needed it to break. The talent to select is such a cruel discriminator. And yet, one feels that the first creature climbing from the sea turned back and noticed something to remember, as if awakening.

When, finally, I leave, the gray has turned to urban darkness slit with lights. It is still raining. And there is no room left in me even for the rain. Once upon a time there was a man who stepped from a gallery into a stormy dusk. And there was not room enough in him even for the rain. It starts that way.

The last thing I recall about my uncle was the day he brought some old movies he had put on video cassettes. Movies strung together from the years around the War. In black and white, in awful light there traipsed his sisters, cousins, people from the neighborhood. Shadowy figures playing at a picnic, nearly hidden by the darker leaves. A frosted cake just on the edge of someone's table. Briefly my father and mother, he in uniform. Others I did not know. I listened to the quibbling over history—*who died in the Pacific. Did his sister marry? No, she drowned after the War, somewhere near Huron.* A future corpse lingered on the screen, smiling uncertainly, leaning in his dark uniform on the darker trunk of an Olds, all the light gathered in his spectacles.

I can imagine my uncle, who was no artist, alone in his basement running the film back over and over, bathed in the spare light of the screen, quibbling with himself in a murmur like a quiet, halting melody, trying to get it all right. Which is, perhaps, why art can speak to anyone.

A Roadside Scene: Mercer, Maine

She turns a little, ducking from
the pulp truck's chilly wake:
devils of bark and dust.

She has draped her girth within two dresses,
both dark green, both worn over
red stretch slacks. K-Mart galoshes,
a coat of hunter's orange.

She moves like a Christmas haystack,
gleaning the frozen brush for bottles,
her face a ruddy paste of slow endurance.
Ten feet away forever, her lean Shepherd
noses the dark, early air,
snapping at his own smoking breath.

Watching him, she stands pure still.
Her rubbish sack, half full,
slips from her hand and opens.

Beyond her the pane of morning light
climbs down the blue mountains.

Early Autumn at Point Judith Light

If you could lose your place anywhere
you could lose it here, with the fog
as lithe as wraiths, with surfers bobbing
on their boards like seals, waiting for just
the perfect crest that will not come, not
this day. A ghostly tern soars in stasis,
tethered to the horn's incessant "No."
But you had dreamed a sycamore, its
own sad mottle, then a lover's tear,
or you had a question or a prayer.
An old question. *What dazzles God's eyes?*
Even these small waves collapse like breaths.

WINTER LAUNDRY

She appears on the wooden porch, her arms filled with a rubbish bag distended with wet laundry. She makes several tries at pulling shut the door with the elbow of her coat before setting down the bag and reaching to the handle. From inside blares the noise of her immunity, her little sons fighting over programs. When she closes the door there is only the sound of wind. Her black coat widens as she bends to lift the bag, to hold it as if it were a huge, soft pumpkin. Her own thickness and the weight of wet clothes and the bitter wind make walking difficult.

She balances her way across the crusted mud of the yard to the laundry line. How little warmth the sun gives. Even the glare from the dead fields hurts her eyes.

Already the clothes are stiff, and she works more quickly than one could believe—pinning the clothes, moving sideways, dragging the bag beside her. The shirts and jeans and towels sway like colored boards. One large sheet is still soft enough to flap. She is nearly done. Wind tears the water from her eyes that, like her visible flesh, seem to have no color at all.

The empty sand truck highballs around the curve like an orange bull gone mad, veers to the shoulder and raises the dust to a cresting wave. Then, more of a cloud, the rising cumulus of dirt hesitates, bursts across her yard. She coughs twice and turns. Her littlest one is yelling through the open door.

THE ARSONISTS

Who knows why the wiring chose that midnight in March to open itself so completely to the wooden frame. Stoney's Antiques & Italians was no more. Just a few charred beams and everywhere the grey, feathery ash coating debris, and the oasis of mud which formed in the crusted snow.

By the time the tanker had arrived there was nothing to do but watch the fire burn itself out like a dying star. The seven firemen, Stoney, Stoney's wife Cecile, and various neighbors ringed the flames, and were transfigured by them so that, had they looked, they could have seen the fire piercing one another like dancing fluoroscopes, their dark organs suddenly astral, as if they had been sharing a tribal dream.

Next day Stoney's cousin Lawrence, walking in the warm rubble, found a lump which had been Topper the cat. Right then Stoney put forth that a mouse may have been gnawing a wire, thinking it was some kind of black cheese. Poof! "Line of duty," he said to Cecile, whose cat Topper had been.

Stoney put on ten pounds he didn't need waiting for the insurance to pay off. He mentioned every time he met someone: "It weren't the building, it were the contents what most hurt." Still, by June the grass was growing back beneath the skeleton of the C&S Dairy Cup. This after Cecile had threatened a divorce over miniature golf and pony rides. And she got another cat on the sly. While Stoney saw the world expanding to accommodate his notions, Cecile felt the closing in of things, the way a yard seemed smaller when lived in long enough. They began to move past each other without speaking, valences of hope and despair which had no present tense.

Stoney built picnic tables for the business, haunting the entire yard, wanting to be open by the Fourth. Cecile moved in a tighter orbit—knitting, rocking, shelling peas, painting a toppings list with red enamel. Both staring away from the center of their gravities, that point at which their eyes no longer met.

Had not. Not since that night of the demonic mouse when they stood watching, feeling the windless flames eating a part of themselves they could not see. It was different. Stoney read the skies all spring, predicting tourists like grain. Cecile saw winter beyond all that, her own blank dreams. As if the flames had altered their eyes, as if they had left the night from different ends. There was nothing to say. That, they spoke in their bones.

RENASCENCE ON MT. BATTIE

And, through and over everything,
A sense of glad awakening.
　　　—"Renascence" Edna St. Vincent Millay

The fog below, the clouds above, the mists between.
I remember well the times when that pewter lens
Was all this altitude revealed. So I looked,
As always, within it for the way beyond.

On that day of unexpected clarities
From atop the mountain we could see
The whole reach of Penobscot Bay
Where the sun could shift its shape across
The waters, the islands once so close,
So familiar, dispersed like children,
The spruce dark mysteries no one solves.

One winter a friend and I had paddled out for lunch.
There was a cabin crumbling to its cellar.
Some logs and blocks, a rotting squirrel.
But the shafts of light between the trees
Speckled down on everything. We almost spoke.
But suddenly the wind came back northeast,
And we beat hell for home like frightened prey.
Later there was time to wonder what we'd learned.
All of that was someone else's life now long ago.

Once in summer, I made the climb alone,
Tracing the very steps *she* took between
The sun and the footfalls of shadows
In ghostly firs, as if bracketing a line
That quivers between hope and desolation.
From there that water that could terrify
Seemed quiet as a mirror. It may be
The oldest tale: water, stone and wood,
The light, the dark, and those who see.

So many years ago, I left a cruel interment
In the valley of the Carrabassett, a daughter gone,
Her hope extinguished by a patch of ice,
The dark trees welcoming beneath the stars.
Christmas looming. It happens that way.

When I was so alone, I used to listen for the silence
Between carols on the radio. Waiting. As if
Each soul would find the moment
To seek ransom from its captive life.
I think that *she* might understand.

That sunny day atop the mountain,
We crouched where *she* would crouch to contemplate
A life as open and as fearsome as the Bay.
Lights on the rocks like words,
Burning even on the glyphs of lichen.

Tonight the snow is spinning, and we are home
In Ohio, almost a universe away. I should know.

I do not need a photograph to see your smile,
To feel your hand half around my waist.
A night ago I watched you light a little candle.
I wanted to say something. I have stories
Like candles, but I decided just to watch and wait.
I think I know the tricky craft of hopefulness.

"Look one way and the sun is going down,
Look the other and the moon is rising."

"Father, do we go to heaven,
Or does it come to us?"

But thinking makes nothing quite so potent
As the breaths we share. Tonight they wind above
Our shoulders like a prayer. A prayer is
A story, too. I think that *she* might understand.

SUN AND MOON WITH WOUNDED SWAN

Here, your wounded voice floats hours
past the telephone, caught like a dream
in the interstices of wind and light,
a wish whose slow accumulation we can see.

So listen, that tender habit something
so like love, like hopefulness,
and search the sky above
the brooms of swaying reeds
and find the sun and moon—
a blazing hand, a faded coin—
balanced in the vacant blue.

It means something, as if standing
in some larger soul's geometry,
the lone swan drifting, its torn wing
slumped an inch or two, unable
to conceal the dark brown sash of injury.

Still, tilted as a broken bob,
it dips to eat the grasses
while in a line across its tail
two others struggle in a slow ascent,
their wing beats like a bellows.

Will you listen with me
to the morning as it paddles near?
A blade of grass dangling
from its beak, its eyes like anthracite.

Lavorando Nel Coure Solo
—For Leonard Craig

So you understand that it is difficult,
working in the heart alone.
The lights among that scrub of birch
that lure you to the river,
the moonlight froth of paper sliding to the sea.
Say it once again to make it real: *Kennebec,*
as three mergansers glide above the jams.
Or is it still the Arno, dark as blood across the hours?

Where is that cottonwood playing in the wind?
And whose eyes, whose poplars like tongues?
There is always too much to see.
Once upon a time there was a woman
who became a cloud within a mist,
with something like a hand to ask the sky.
There might have been a moon, a name.
But she was never yours. There was a boy
near a well, a cross of cedar painted gold.
Memory's a mirror to leave unfinished.

She could have risen near the lines of hay
spilled from a wagon. She could have risen
from the limestone gurgling like an angel.
It could have started with her wrist across a pillow.
What can a moment know for sure?
Once you stood in silence in the grotto of a saint.
Once you let the morning sun remind you
of a *pomodoro* she left rotting in the oil.
You wait until the stories change enough.

So linger beside some singing water
that is never quite sufficient, not for you.
Walk among the strangers who seek explanations.
Show them something anyway.

THE WAITING PLACES

Advent at the Port of Galilee

Not for the first time does he linger in his car
as the sun's last flare is extinguished in
the black Sound. Across the lot behind him
two diners gaze from George's window, where
lights are blinking on a little tree,
carols that make the waitress hard to hear.
A lone purse seiner churns through darkness
on the rising tide. The running lights
reveal the slicker of a man astern
who is bent a little, coiling something.
Across the way some windows light Jerusalem.
Perhaps he does not need God to make
something out of nothing after all.
A day ago, a year ago, perhaps today,
he drove above the frozen Mohawk Valley,
down there crows drifted to the snow
like parachutes. Once he told a lover
he was coming home across these mountains,
floating like a bubble in the wind.
He doesn't need the stars,
and tonight there are none.
To be this perfectly alone is so much
like the start of one thing or another
that it feels like a choice.
If he cracks his window, he can hear
the fading slap of the seiner's wake.
He remembers that he loved her face,
candled by the moon, as much when he saw it
as when he did not. It was there, waiting.
Perhaps hope is just his situation.
It could have been a seal, that water's kiss,
the black eyes cradling someone's light
as if it might just shatter.

TRUE AND UNTRUE AT CHRISTMAS

On this morning, of all mornings, he could not
remember any lie he'd ever told.
But sitting at the table in his ex-wife's kitchen
and staring up the slope of the yard,
he can watch a red-tail warring with some crows
above the broken cans of Genny Lite
his son had stacked beneath a yew.
They had been targets for his grandson's
Christmas rifle and glitter now
like melted ornaments.

Alone at the table he stares absently,
his own hands somehow as red
as if he had been busy pawing snow.
From another room he hears a radio.
He knows that he's not welcome here.

Of course, once upon a time, there was
a brother who stole his food, his money,
then his sight, and then his soul. And so
he clasped his life from tree to tree,
or so the story goes. At last he found
the whiskey dripping from an oak,
like the sweet fire of the whole world.

He used to use the mornings for forgiveness.
Last night, among his family, he had crooned
his own old song of explanation
*That was my territory—all the way
from Binghamton to Hammondsport.*
It is the music that he knows by heart.

As for the rest, he would simply tell you
that his love was always too large
or too small for his family to bear.

If the light in his bourbon resembles
the light in his eyes, such an old story
is worth a quiet curse or two.

But it's Christmas morning, and a sliver
of sunlight plays upon the targets.
The birds have fled, and he is still here,
like something left behind a sigh.

ADVENT FROM THE BLUE WATER BRIDGE

Today I drive across the span of someone's hope,
the one that happened. Two million vehicles a year,
whose people all see something here.
Today a single freighter sorties north
into Huron's wide and frigid blue
toward a promise of the Soo...and then?
While south across the land's gray stew
where nothing is as once it was
the stack-plumes bend as white as bones
in the same wind that sings from rigging,
"The year is nearly gone, and we shall see..."

In a week, if the ship is safe for then,
resting in Duluth, its cargo traded,
its sailors murmuring in dreams
under quilts and wreaths and stars, can we say
that life has kept a bargain with a few?

Two million vehicles a year,
whose people all see something here,
and in each a moment waits
when we're stopped by what we see
and left to wonder, *"Whose hope was this?"*
Below, the shops are lit with expectation.
And yet we always wish for good beyond each end.
My father told me stories.
So somewhere, still, the Interurban cars
have chimed and slowed, their passengers
about to dance among the platform's snows.

What might they make of this construction?
It's so familiar, the way our souls
adsorb to steel and stone
and make our wishes over things we see.
I watch that solitary vessel counting miles
as the whitecaps build. From its deck
I'm lost into the eastern sky beneath a star.
It is a story that we tell.

In Advent
—For Louis Adams 1919-1998

From the bridle trail, whitetail flash
among the trees and disappear. Or perhaps
the low sun glances off the scruffy barks.
Each version has its possibilities
as something fills the blank desire
to be a story we believe in
because we can recall a moment when
the deer were real, or the plays of sun
on one tree more particular.

Is it only human to imagine
that each story has its shadow
just as true? Nature gives us
only what we glean, a thing to hope for.

When the tide leaves, the sand emerges
with its worn or broken flotsam
lost or found by accident.
When the sun bleeds into the night's black silt
we wake the stars. We think,
"If not one thing, then another..."

A year ago, waiting for my father,
I watched a mother and her daughter
leave oncology, silent as willows,
their baggy woolen caps a powdered blue,
the petals of their awful skin
reflected in the doors as amber.
Their taxi vanished in the Cleveland rain.

I caught his eyes, and for the first time in my life
that I didn't know the answer
I asked him if he were afraid. *No.*

My arm still lifts him from the sheets to drink.
This trail winds near the stream
whose pools he ran to as a wild boy.
The color of his mother's plum trees in a dream.

Father, even hope is a construction
as you knew so perfectly.
Last night Orion walked above me,
a story that you showed me long ago.

Each day, each place, I set these memories
like cairns that mark your simple gift
of what to hope for, how to be. As if
we were the children of our own brief lives.

ADVENT GRAVES AT ALL SOULS CEMETERY

It seems that I am walking on a frozen steppe
and not this rolling country east of home.
The distant cedars breathe and spin the snow
as filigrees. The stone evangelists each gaze
upon a corner of this plat I know by heart.

For a little while the rules are slackened to allow
the varnished crosses, the wreaths with crimson ribbons,
the linen orchids and chrysanthemums.
One grave even has a small, blue chimney
with a stocking and a photograph—a boy in khaki.
It feels like a riot of remembrance without words.

I wouldn't lie about such things, not in
this sacred ground in which the syllables
of Eastern Europe sleep in their last America.

They need two wolves to howl and prance
a *Czárdás* and remember—the wedding
dances on linoleum, the lamps and sparks
and whirring lathes consigned unto
the last shifts of their lives, in which
the yellow buses growl past TAPCO,
Eaton Axle, Fisher Body, Chase Brass—
all grown filmy as the cloud of toil and beads
from cuts that drip into the lubricating oil.
The morning songs of beer and cabbage and anger.

It was that cloud they shared he couldn't bear
and couldn't breathe. For years I watched him
wander to each labor as if searching for his tribe.

The wind stings my neck and scrapes across the graves.
Can I stand here as the better life he dreamed?
I know that forty years ago we left a job

as numb as ice and watched the winter sun
plunge beneath the Cuyahoga's purple ridge
to leave behind a single star I still hold near.
Waiting there or here, it is my only answer.

ADVENT AT THE LOOKING GLASS RIVER

He seldom dreams of what he sees,
but the streetlamp's moon is growing in his eyes
like an orchid that the world flows past.
He stares at the black mirror of the river
until the stars appear at last.

From up the hill the carols float to him
among the bursts of snow.
White dwarves, red giants—is each
an angel still, all in flight beyond their names?

Once he thought to watch would be enough;
a watcher never lacks a reason, never needs a dream,
as if the story by itself could heal—
the boy spilling wax upon the cassock
is saved as is the thief, if only…

He helped his father tie the boughs to wreaths.
Another, dreaming, says to his friend,
"Did you see the old man on the bridge?"

He seldom dreams of what he sees,
but the darkness that he wakes to is familiar.
Outside the locusts still join hands upon the snow,
and the crows that watched him home
sleep in pines without a wish.

In the dream the boy says, "Father, do we
go to heaven, or does it come to us?"
In the room his dog sighs once
and closes its black eyes.

An Advent Dream Begins in Majuro

This sheeting squall has draped a shroud
upon such lights that were as watch fires moored
across the black lagoon, a perfect darkness.
Last night, waiting for a ride I caught instead as glimpse
a pickup streaming, hung with boughs of ironwood,
a plastic reindeer wrapped with strings of lights
and strapped atop the cab. The driver, in profile,
showed a grin that still escapes description,
and I remember how it is to be a stranger anywhere.

Once it was walking the frozen stubble
marking last year's corn, beside the black ice
of a drainage ditch, watched by crimson eyes
atop a distant silo. Once it was a red clay right of way while
the CHESSIE rumbled northward as its own terrifying wind.

And now, as the squall has fled,
some wondrous silence as the world is reconstructed
from abyss—coral heads like patens in the moonlight,
the ships and fires, the dark straw of the islets.

I've heard it said that there is no dream of *now*, but still I
wonder. Wake and sweep a hand across the longitudes, and
walk with the ghosts my mother sees,
lying in her frailty where *now* is one more breath.

Once it was to lean against an elm and watch the hunter
climb its winter limbs, a story just impossible.
What a thing it is, even happiness, this waiting!
Remember how it is to be a stranger anywhere,
or a man with a reindeer on his cab.

A Hunter in a Tree Stand: Allegany County

The Southern Tier Expressway falls beneath
the ridges deepened by the paltry sun.
There a tongue of fire girds a maple
and grows into a man whose shotgun
rests across his knees, his whole repose
like a sad gourd hardened to eternity.

For he has waited hours, that is, for years
while the snow has drifted trackless
in the clearing ringed with pine because,
as he is now a memory,
he has remembered through the empty hours
what his patience yields—if not
his target, then his life.

Now, from his window, he follows
as his mother sings the steaming cows
into the barn, and the frozen mud
is laced with straw. Her red hand
high against the door has found
his forehead raging with the flu.

One autumn when the sky was maize
his uncle led him to the woods
and showed him how the pines
reveal the wind he could not feel.

His stand is perfect, but the deer to which
he is a death as random as a memory
has not appeared. He curls his toes,
tucks his hands inside his coat,
and rocks so slightly with a tender moan
that is swallowed by the distant whine
of tires on the road.

THE TRACE OF HOPE FROM LOCK 29

Lock 29 on the old Ohio & Erie Canal was an aqueduct
that raised the canal boats above the bending stretch of
the Cuyahoga River at the village of Peninsula, Ohio.
Remnants of the old lock remain.

He shuffles through December rain that is waiting to be snow,
waiting to be darkness. The river winds and bubbles,
today its power more a rumble than a roar.
He stands before the remnants of the lock that lifted
the canal boats high across the river's coils.

If he were not alone, someone might hear him whisper
"The river is a path, the canal is a path, and then
the water's voices, too." All paths that lead
to last night's dream, with his question to
a cloud above his bed: *How am I to love all things*
laid before me at this age of counting losses, in such a world as this?
Lovers, friends and creatures—all consigned to memories.
Hopefulness has always been his answer,
but now the favored scripture passes from his lips
like a habit worn out from its use.
              Lord I believe…

They built this canal to tame the waters,
but no water is ever tamed for good.
The canals fell to the rails, that fell to roads,
that swelled to highways. Each chance buried in another's hope.
In any case he is standing here alone, once the hope of two,
waiting at the mossy lock as if it were a sepulcher.

Long ago, in a time of sorrow, a country pastor
told him "Think of the present imperfect.
Be emptying your hopes of everything but hope.
Figure it out. You will be okay."

He remembers two years ago exactly,
Driving back down Riverview, dazzled
by sunlight slanting through a stand of cedars
Like a fold of angels. But that was then.
Now the rain has found its temperature.
In the darkness graupel dances on his hood
and in his lights, sparking in the darkness.
He is drifting to the boy in the back seat
of a Mercury, staring at the Christmas lights,
his breath a halo on the glass, the soft voices of assurance.
The snow becoming fire, becoming stars.
He is thinking he will be okay.

Advent in a COVID Year
The cure for loneliness is solitude.
—Marianne Moore

Good poet, I must beg to differ,
Especially in this year when our lives became
More dangerous than even we could dream.

Dawn has turned my yard to monochrome,
The snow from yesterday pocked by clumps
Of leaves that form the surface of a moon.
But more than season speaks of waiting.

In this long year of loneliness, my lover
Metamorphosed to a stone of *now*
That one might touch yet never reach,
Dark magic with no "true apothecary."
My friends die off like ancient trees
Snapped at last by living's winds, marked
In some accounting book I cannot see.

And yet, last week I watched three horses
Turned to pasture. At first, they sprinted each
To corners of the field, then slowly drifted
Toward a center, as if remembering themselves.
They nickered, pawed, and shook their manes.
And then these strong and fearsome animals,
With happy teeth and lips and tongues,
Began to groom each other's heads and flanks.
It seems that only creatures can speak tenderness.

Within a night of sleep, a dream of stone and snag,
I watched again my father climb a ladder,
stringing boughs and lights for our whole town.
In those auras he looked down at me.
Catch a snowflake on your tongue,
And you will have it all your life.

Twenty years ago in Michigan, I watched
A townsman hanging lights upon a bridge
That crossed the Looking Glass River
And penned these lines: "Father, do we go
To Heaven/Or does it come to us?"
In that dream he said it was a prayer.
Now I sense that prayer is more
A trade of breaths than pleading of desires.
Hier bin í. Da, bist du.[1]
As the sun begins to lift a little, and
The world brings color to its frames again,
Drawing near such scenes that I can add
To memory—seeking there my hopefulness.
Here I am. It is enough.

---

1 These words ("Here I am./There you are.") appear in Randall Jarrell's poem "A Game at Salzburg," in which he casts them as an exchange between ourselves and God. Make of that what you will.

ADVENT AND THE BLESSINGS OF CROWS

He is stopped at the end of the offramp
as the cars stream by in both directions. Waiting.
He lifts his eyes to the field across the road,
a collage of scrub and yellow clay.
Then he sees the crows, sagging the limbs
of three dark and leafless trees.

There must be near a hundred, shimmering
like black candle flames. In that moment
before he hears the horn, he wonders
at their calculations. Three will light
as four depart, climbing slowly north
into a haze with clouds of rose and gold.

Driving on, he counts the measures
of such movements, until he comes upon
two crows picking at the carcass of a squirrel.
It happens as it does because it does.
Those crooked trees that only crows would seek
become a constellation mapped across his soul.

He stops a while to ponder in the Cuyahoga Valley,
parking in the lot above the Quarry Lock, where
failing sunlight flashes through a stand of cedar.
Lights and shadows as ethereal as his grasp
of hopefulness. He steps out and haunts
the shadow lines to better see the airs.

In his mind the crows still light and leave.
He thinks, "How they roost in our propensities!"
They bring wisdom. They bring fear. They tell futures.
They chant the story of creation.
Or maybe they're just busy being crows.
He's heard it said that crows can dream.

He's heard it said that crows have memories
that crowd their *now* with how to live.
He waits and he remembers. It is a season
to hear the rising tones of crows at dawn,
at gloaming, in their Book of Hours.
And there he sighs without a trace of gloom.

MATTERS OF THE HEART

A Story about Love at Tenant's Harbor

When you have become familiar with the shore at Tenant's Harbor, there are things in which you must believe. Last night, from the window of the only room she has called her own, she imagined that the half-moon nested in the dark spruce had blessed her wish. And for all it matters, maybe it did. At least that is how she walks this morning, past his pickup idling by the buckets of menhaden.

She sees him at the end of the pier, coiled purple with rage, his right arm slicing air, cursing at a man she cannot see. On that arm the ragged bracelet she had woven from old line, and beyond that the water rippling with the sunlight broken like jewels. She had wished his shyness meant he must be gentle. But he has learned too well already to trust only what obeys, and he curses past her as she ducks the hand that doesn't come.

He slams the door and burns the tires, tumbling off the thermos she had brought for them to share. You can see him staring at her shrinking in the mirror, her hands as empty as the air. Her face is red as a sunset. Yes, she is crying, too, but even that is muted by the squawks of ordinary gulls.

SNAKE TRAIL METAMORPHOSIS

"The horse knows when you know, and he knows when
you don't know."
"The horse is never wrong."

—Ray Hunt

At the lifting of the rein he gives a little snort
That almost seems a sigh, as if he knows
The trail to love is near impossible.
His step is heavy with uncertainty
As we struggle to find this thing, this feel.
Right rear, left front. Left rear, right front.
Repeated now as if it were a chant until
The footfalls of the trot can disappear,
And only heart remains. I count the only words
That I had left to give you.
La querida con todo mi corazón.

The heartbeats sink into the ground like wishes,
Like witches, and rise as monarchs glowing
Orange within the skylights. *Right rear, left front.*
Left rear, right front. Find the feet and find the feel.
Only then is it permissible to dream.

In this moment I would tell you all these things,
But now you say we don't exist.
Right rear, left front. Left rear, right front.
A search both endless and elusive

Later, I'll remember my mistakes.
Later I will feel the counting of your heart
Even though you don't exist.
In the same way I remember redwings buzzing
In the corn beneath a molten core of sun.
It seems the present moment also tracks
Some histories. It was August. It was an age ago.

It was not us, but just an ordinary miracle,
Like that sliver of a moon upon your ear.
The trail to love is near impossible.

Now, this horse is doubtless wondering if I am
Any use at all in making something clear.
He simply stops there in his tracks
To make me listen. It seems that he and I
Possess the mercy gift of waiting.

And so, I wait for you, knowing it's in vain.
Right rear, left front. Left rear, right front.
Counting steps to help enfold
The helpless dream of loving with a feel.

GIVING THINGS AWAY
—for Mary Jarrell and Terri Strug

I'm never certain if they come
as friends or strangers, those moments
when you begin to see things differently.

Today I had my oldest friend for tea.
I faced her with my good eye to the window,
near the white geranium.
An oriole changed branches in the dogwood.
What could be more ordinary?

She stirred the cream as always,
her spoon ringing on the gilded lip.
I thought the cake she brought was dry
as she folded her napkin with a breath,
and said, "You know, your life
stares out at us from every shelf."

I stared at her tepid, brown eyes
that used to burn across men's hearts.
It's not just we who seem to shrink.
The world in which we lived departs like starlight
looking back at us—thinner, smaller each day.

Last night I spent the gloaming counting things—
the portraits with the rosewood frames;
the tiny, lead eland, its forelegs crossed
as if in waiting; the witch
carved from a linden bough—I remember

how she glared and followed like a wind—
my mother's damask packed in cedar;
a little cask of broaches and pins...
all of it too much like evidence. At dawn
I filled my cheeks with rouge.

I told her it was long past time
we started giving things away.
That for her, this for him...whom to trust
with what was dear? Did I say *was*?
That bird preened itself in the window's mirror.

It's so odd. Tonight I tried to count
the vanities I've owned, and wondered
what to do with blue, silk gloves
from an aunt I hardly knew,
the one from Sarasota who went mad
from poisoning the crows...

I thought, am thinking now,
really, there's just so little to decide.
It's too much like the first gray hair.

So instead I watched the April sunlight
peeling low beneath the awning,
and pointed to that poplar by the road.
"When a storm comes, the leaves
wave like little silver hands."

A Love Scene

It was still early in August, but already summer was leaving Frenchman's Bay. He could see it in the silver haze offshore, feel it in the cold hull of his kayak, remember the asters popping everywhere on shore. Late in afternoon, and the sun had started its slow path down the sky. He turned the boat back towards Hull's Cove and the cottage he had rented for a couple days. He knew that Sugar, his Border Collie, would be waiting restlessly, probably with her legs crossed. It was not easy to find a little place near the water that would take a pet.

About a hundred yards from shore he noticed two women leave their cottage and start walking to the shore. As they and he grew closer he noticed they were walking leaned into each other, an arm around each other's waist. One had long blond hair braided almost to her waist. The other a redhead with a kind of bowl cut just below her ears. The offshore breeze carried the notes of their voices, if not the words. Suddenly a bit uncomfortable, and not sure why, he decided to maneuver a little further down the shore to land the boat. He drifted gently in, parallel to the pebbly shore to protect the hull. His back now to the couple, he braced his paddle on a little reach of soil and climbed from the boat.

He stood staring back at the Bay, letting his legs come back under him. The women, behind him, had lapsed to silence. He lifted the boat and hung the coaming on his shoulder, which turned him toward the spot where they were sitting, near a clump of beach roses and the dark skeleton of an old jetty. The women turned to him and smiled, and he nodded in return. He felt a bit like an intruder and carried the boat the eighty yards or so to the step of his cottage and set it on the grass.

Sugar was ready, of course, and burst from the door as soon as he opened it. She ran around him in a circle before pacing off to find her spot. He sat on the step. Despite himself, he stared down to the couple at the shore. He could barely hear their laughter, but he could see it. The blonde reached up and stroked the other's hair with a tenderness that made him sigh. Far out on the bay, a white sail heeling just a little.

He asked himself if this was love he saw and answered *what else could it be*. People seeking solitude for different reasons. So long he had sought what he was seeing now. He got up and went inside to start some coffee. Sugar followed to plead for dinner. The little stove brought him to the window where they were in his view, framed by the red-checked curtains. He took one more glance and turned away. He sensed they had something to savor and would still be there as the shadows on the bay walked their way to shore.

First Light

It is not like mercy when it comes,
this that we call light.
For the flowers in it die in ways
too ordinary—like something spilled across a sill.
It seems we must name everything.

What would we dream without windows?
Wake to watch the blackbirds fly into the sun,
to hear the willows brush the air like sand.
In another room a *scherzo* fades to static.
For hours no one comes; it is so like life.

Once it began with the paper rasp of leaves
crumbling underneath my shoes,
the broken shale as blue
as the moon watched through sycamores.

To wait for words in the bar's soft fire
is to see you again for the first time,
your hair longer, tumbled down a sweater.
Later you said you were an actor at heart,
staring at the amber of the lager.
So I watched you forge your tear
into a ring and throw it to the sea.

It is October; it is morning.
The boy whose story you will hear
is burning leaves, a bandana in his hand
as he whispers to the embers.
His dog is frozen at his side, eyes like black pearls.
Well, it was just a story anyway.

Let it be the moment on the porch's swing
when your daughter slowly climbs into your arms.
When you've emptied every lullaby,
and there's nothing to remember.
Just open your hand.

Lessons from the Barn

She strokes his blaze, and his lips will quiver.
It seems so simple. As she has so many times,
she whisks the horsefly from his withers
with a hand as quick as starlight.

For a decade they have had this conversation.
Dancing on the longe line, walking beside him
with the lead, brushing out the winter dirt
as the drifts sweep through the open door,
shaping spirits to a likeness only they can know.
Once she was sure she woke to see him
on a hillock of black grasses, a breathing
silhouette against the broken rainbow of a dawn.

She could walk to him there, the chestnut
hearts of his eyes floating to her open hands.
For such moments they have fled the splinters
and the snags of elsewhere. In one bad dream
that staggered into real, she had nearly
lost him to a dollar's hungry shadow.

But not now. In the ring he glides beneath her
at the canter, peers both forward and behind.
To watch them balanced on the turn
is to see she has him on the perfect lead
into the pasture of her undiscovered soul,
where there is no measure to her smile.
It is there that they navigate
both their solace and their joy.

AT THE CLEARVIEW

Where is our fulcrum here, as the backlights
Of the bar shine red and gold through rows
Of liquors, and the long day's rains still slap
Against the windows? The latest hard news
Tells its story in your eyes. I watch you
Try to relish your salmon and your wine.

For ten weeks you've borne everything but agony
Without a tear that anyone could see:
The waiting rooms, the scans, the therapies,
The weeks inside a walker, constant pain.
Now it all dissolves in a flood of sobs.

I rush to hold you as the other faces
Rise or look away. You lean into me
As if we could disappear in our own
Shadows. *We will get through this, yes, we will.*
We walk into a night that just might
See us differently, mocking hope or joy.

What can I give you here that must remain?
Some words are flowers; some are stones; others
Shimmer, fade like ghosts we can't remember.
Dìgame Nada! Nothing is enough.
We drive away, your good hand on my knee,
Making what we can from nothing at all.

A WIDOW'S LETTER TO HER DAUGHTER

I sit alone on this Sunday night
with the sun a broken saucer
spun beneath a palm
whose fronds reflect an orange
more ancient than my cast of memory.

Below, the people on the boardwalk seem so *ordinary*,
no one singular enough to mark,
and so I'm left with no defenses
adequate to staunch the tide of recollection.

You could listen…
The surf is gentle and insistent
like a child's rhyme, its syncopation
resonant as birds before a storm.

When is the last time that I sent a letter?
I waited for an hour to begin this page.
I know you cannot read my words
without aversion,
for my habit is to criticize a life
you have defined until we live, almost,
in different hemispheres.

Oh, there's a pelican
planted in the surf like marble.

There, now I can say something
that I notice because of you.
But what to make of it…
This morning I bought jonquils
at the mini mall, the one
where you wired shut your jaw
when I told you what looked good on you.
That place with pastel lions, and
the macaw Jenny taught to say goodbye.

Something in me catches on that memory.
Can't just remembering be worth something?
For years we've had little more than ways
to say goodbye, smiles like ornaments.
The last time that you called
I spent an hour talking furniture,
and I could almost see you drifting,
and so I asked for Jenny
as if to pull the line a little shorter.
How careful can a mother be?

Because I tell imperfect lies
with such ferocity, I'm left
with that confusion in your eyes
each time we chance upon
that thing I know alone,
the trail of its telling cold
as dead explorers at the pole.

When he died, I remember
standing on the stairs,
gazing down the sable banister.
How the carpet seemed to eat the light,
how a thousand drafts emerged.

That broken night I lay in bed
and watched the frosts illuminate
the blackened panes, so long ago
became a mantra, one I've whispered
nearly every waking hour.
No... No... No... No...

You quoted someone once:
"The heart has eyes as well..."
At least, I remember that you did.
And now, somehow, we're older
than either of us could have thought.
I'm writing what I cannot say.
I know how hard I've looked away.
I know. Here, just now, the sun is gone.

And two lovers walk below,
slowly down the sand—
who else would melt that way?

Lost at the Grand Haven Light

They walked along the breakwall,
with their shoes in hand, dodging bursts of spray,
to sit on blocks beyond the lighthouse.

Near them, a mother comes unglued with fear
grasps the air behind her daughter's hand.
One boat balances on swells to make the harbor.

She stares, unblinking, west across the waves,
where a single purple cloud appears.
He'd thought for sure her eyes were brown.

Gazing at the lights of water in the pitted stone,
he slides his foot to brush her toes
as her leg recoils like a startled bird.

A Semi-Private Room

It's getting darker though I just can't tell
how long I've been awake this time.
Every clock I've ever seen has hands
that look as if they're meant to kill,
but this fluid dripping into me
reminds me of a clock I saw once
as a girl in school, its hands
like goldfish swimming over pennies.

I'm told the tumor they took out of me
looked like a fruit, and someone
ate it in the lab to prove by laughter
I might live awhile.
A doctor comes and goes
like someone waiting to be thanked.

Behind the curtain Mary snores
and groans in her narcotic dream,
but this morning she could laugh
at us two mothers "brought in for repairs."
This morning she still had her foot.
A shadow there's her sister Gwendolyn,
who holds her hand as if it were a throw.

Sometime today my Jimmy comes to see me
looking shaggy as a garden
someone planted and forgot to tend.
But that's not possible—
he was my first most careful sadness,
and his liquors like a storm that
I felt coming as he sets the chocolate
on my table. *Such a handsome boy.*
You must be proud.
His recognition is a sudden draft.
He leans against the radiator,
half staring out the window.

We trade our silence for description
as he tells me how the dirty shore ice
shatters into little bergs,
the water and the sky the same gray
that a house sees in a nightmare.
I think, "The things he sees!"
He hesitates in a love
he wants me to define
and carry like an extra skin.

Let the ice go, let the water
where it wishes; none of it is mine.

I feel as if the scalpel meant to save me
cut across the lines that held me to my life.
Now where? Counting here how often
fish swim back and forth across my eyes
until the nurse comes with two paper cups:
one for water, one for pills.
She is careful as a spider
and it's the care that frightens me.

When it's dark and I've awakened,
his shift has ended, Jim is here,
and someone's put his red carnations
in a vase beside my pillow.

I know after some moments
he will move beside the bed
and ask me how I feel in the same voice
he'd ask anything, brushing
his stiff palm across my soft one.

For thirty years we've bartered visitations,
like pulling one another up a ladder.
We've worked so hard at helping
all I think of is how tired I am...
If I could wake up in a month or so,
I know that I might love him once again.
But now, awake, I wonder what else
he has grown in me like spies.

I can't erase the breath I gave
so long ago a second sooner than I should.

All this from, *yes*?
So one by one they tell me,
"Just get better." Was I meant
to teach them how to love me,
to love anyone?

In my missal there's a dead carnation
and a holy card I've kept for years,
where Jesus' crown is wound around his heart.
I once confessed that in a dream I saw
a card where Mary's heart had eaten His
and spit the thorns out in the dust.
If I could sit up higher, I could see
the weather as it boils up from the lake,
snowflakes spinning up and down
outside the window, lost as possibilities.

Those snowflakes are not prayers
or angels, just cold ashes
of some flowers brought me long ago.
To see the goldfish one more time
could mean I'm crazy, or I've died.
To see my son, my husband…
it could mean that if someone
hears me pray tonight, it's for the flowers
not for anything that breathes.

In a Children's Gallery

The dark print of your skirt
has traced your leg as if
it were a pond on which
I breathed your name,
but you have simply moved
among the children's art
to find your daughter
while I wait and wander
by the walls hung
with the cubes and deltas,
the troubled stars
of their dreams, and I think
in the tongues of gods and children
words of a doom as ecumenical as dawn.

Is that your voice?

Once upon a time
I saw a painting of a crane
above the forks of pale grasses,
on its wing a poem
that said this crane
would climb to heaven
with the moon in its beak
like a pearl.

WALKING TO THE MOON

It floats a foot above the line of poplars.
So familiarly pale, so accessible
they might go there, she prays,
just crossing the gulf of air,
climbing the wings of fireflies.

It is their moon, these lovers,
lighting the blue hands of the wheat,
the white asters he had braided in her hair
above the cloak they wear as one
to hide their hands.

He slows to blend their steps
as playful chimes of voice
soften to no more than breath.
Turning to him, she feels the wool
slip off her shoulder,
a sudden feather of the night.

Near, a dog has rolled upon their path
and risen as a moment of ice,
believing what it sees.

RICORDI

ALONG THE KENNEBEC

Here in Hallowell, the leaving sun
Climbs spruce and pine along the river,
Turns the ebbing tide to ink beneath
The window where we order supper.
I knew the day had tired you, but if
Anywhere in Maine could surprise us
With Pad Thai that you might love, surely
It's in Hallowell, where this river,
My ancient friend, glides to bless our lives.

A WINDOW IN NARRAGANSETT

You left my bed seven hours ago.
Your scent still haunts the sheets, the pillows.
Through my window a willow's curtains
Sway in the night's breath, seem to toss
Our lives. We sought such things with longing.
Knowing, not knowing. I remember
Your fingers at play, their fall, their lie.
I have no heart to change anything.

TO THE DENTIST

The faint moon sinks west behind the trees
That crest this valley's wall. From the east
The sun has lit the snow on fire. And
I am seeking you again down this
familiar road, for the dentist now.
In the old Tomb of the Medici
Michelangelo cast the dawn as
Woman. How could he have seen you then,
So perfect, stretched upon your pillow?

166

Perhaps

Perhaps in winter we read too much.
Last night I had a failed dream—trying
to imagine Crete in February. But even
in the land of dreams I had no clue.
No stooping olive trees, no ancient wells.
"These crazy Americans…why do they
wish to die on top of everything?"
I'll go to the desert. It's winter there, too,
The hermits can hear God alone. Go crazy alone.

Father

Father, the last time I stood at your grave
a bitter wind raked the autumn grasses,
tumbled flowers down that gentle hill.
Now the melting snow is dripping from my eaves,
a sort of breathing. I never told you…
driving through a Pennsylvania spring,
the hills flush with a tender rust
of crab apples, of sumac, my hand in wind
once more a child's wing. And there you were.

In This Dream

In this dream you leaned back from the table,
writing a story of some life in winter.
"I have not found perfect silence anywhere…"
You said it was a woman writing to her soul.
She wandered along an Erie as quiet as milk.
The gulls said nothing, did not even move
when she crouched to grasp a little eye
of quartz, waited and let it fall without
even a sigh, the sun sinking like a red kite.

A Hummingbird Dreams She is a Raven

Of course a hummingbird can dream.
In her dream the dream comes true.
She began by searching windows for their nectar,
waiting until torpor slowed the blur of tiny wings,
as busy as her breaths, to the dark arc
of the raven's soar.

There she could remember and foresee.
She saw the world in flood. She told the gods
they were betrayed. She stole the stars and earth
and water for her child. He is because of her.
Driving together in her car, he had told her
that she was a hummingbird after all.
But, still, he knows she is his miracle.

Mysterium Amoris

The poet followed his angel to a cave. "You have come to ask
Aphrodite to give you all three forms of love: Philos, Eros, and Agape.
In this cave you see four baskets. One holds those loves you seek.
One holds the void of utter darkness. One holds a deadly serpent.
And one holds all three. Your fate is in the baskets. The choice
is yours, and choose you must, or you will cease to be."
— from the *Tale of the Poet Seeking Love*

1.
It began with a dream of a silver cloud
Mottled with darkened hands
Inviting, haunting, unknowable,
It followed him for all his years
As if it were a weather of his soul.

Once he met a poet friend to talk of love
Within the terror of the State.
They left wondering why and how such joy
Could be so dangerous to everyone.
Petr returned to Olomouc and freedom,
Where he was free to be alone and die alone,
Leaving only poems and dreams behind
For the few who might remember,
A phrase they shared in parting.

He remembered his friend while sitting alone
Upon a granite shelf in Maine,
An August haze above the ocean far below.
He was empty as a bowl turned upside down.
"It happens as it does it does because it does."
A flock of cormorants fluttered past
A spray of crest as he was thinking,
"We become our own because."

2.

To truly love is to be afraid of love.
He wondered who wrote that one.
And yet, she came into his life.
She was herself; she was the cloud,
Fresh in a knockoff Chapel hat,
Her eyes the deepest blue of the Pacific
Formed beyond the reef in Majuro.
Her pains etched in the lines that framed her smile.
The curves that filled her jeans, the voice
That could be any music that she chose.
There was nothing left for him to do but fall
Into the deepest wish he'd ever known.

3.

And yet, and yet, that phrase that troubles wishes
Echoed in their years. It was so easy to fail
In learning how to love. The wrong words, the wrong
Perceptions, the clumsy touch so seeking tenderness.
It could be like landing from the journey of a life
And looking back to see the boats on fire.
Every ecstasy could spark a question,
Shift a mirror to their histories so dense
With doubt that love might break like faith.
The joy of *now*, the fear of *next*.

And yet, and yet, that phrase that troubles doubts,
Could never fade to silence. They were, they weren't
A kind of one, a story of a dream that would not retreat.
She curled him like a flower. He held her as a lover
Until their flesh had steamed a happy sigh.
The joy of *now*, the fear of *next*.

He will sit upon a shelf, waiting alone for her
Until time will drain all possibilities.
He will hear the whispers of her song,
      That weather of his soul.

Home Country

"Looking at a Map of the Midwest Interurban Lines"- I had long been fascinated by trains, having heard their "mournful cry" as I drifted to sleep growing up in Cleveland. The Midwest Interurban trains were an especially intriguing story. One could go all the way from Pittsburgh to Milwaukee on the old lines.

"A Woman in a Trailer Park"- This is more of a "walk into it" poem. I was working with my father on a water line in winter, and I ducked into the rental agent's trailer to get warm. There, I observed this scene. Well, most of it.

"A Domestic Scene"- This poem began with a conversation overheard at lunch. The woman speaking in the poem had been married for many years to a man who was deaf and mute. About 1/3 of the lines here derive from the original conversation. The rest was invention.

"A Gray Not Morning's Eye"- Every once in a while, one stumbles upon magic. Back in the 80s, I was fortunate enough to attend a stunning performance of Prokofiev's *Romeo and Juliet* in Cleveland. The starring roles were danced by Raymond Rodriguez and Karen Gabay, so the dedication. In a rarity for me, I practically wrote the poem in my head while driving home. The title, of course, is from the play.

"From Twelve Cleveland Windows (After Marc Chagall)"- What would poets do without windows? I have been enchanted with Marc Chagall's *Jerusalem Windows* ever since encountering them in a book of plates during grad school. Many years later, I decided to create a set of "Cleveland Windows." Here are three of those windows, composed in a structure honoring the mystical numerology of Chagall's set of windows.

"Where We Came In"- *The Bridges at Toko-Ri* was a film based on a novel by James Michener about a pilot in the Korean War. Bank Night was a kind of give-away promotion sponsored by movie theaters in the Fifties to boost midweek attendance. In those days it was possible to enter the film in the middle and sit through it as many times as you wished. It was my father's practice to do so. In a chilling reminder of the era, even candy was "atomic." The

Rapid Transit train still runs down Shaker Boulevard in Cleveland. The hammer mentioned is an electric jackhammer.

"At the U.A.W. Softball Field"- In the summer of 1973 my father, his buddy and I built a softball field for the union on the property of the Ford engine plant in Brookpark, Ohio.

"Open House at the Cleveland Valve Plant: 1996"- This tour was meant to celebrate an agreement between the union and the management of the ancient TRW Valve Plant, an agreement that would allow the plant to remain open. And it did, just not for long.

"Caught Alive"- I had been in a cave-in while working on a sewer line in bad ground. My father dug me out with his hands and no doubt saved my life. Later, when I tried to cast the experience in a poem, I found I could only do so in third person, and at a level of abstraction beyond the real event.

"At the Industrial Accidents Clinic"- I often compose poems while listening to music. Funny how certain pieces went with certain poems. Here it was the Mozart, with its strange shifts of mood, at least to my ear.

County Roads

"County Road No. 5"- One of a series of poems was written over many years trying to capture some of the elements of rural isolation in the stark and wondrous landscapes of northwest Ohio. The naming convention of the poems came from the tradition of having rural roads with numbers rather than names. I was looking for a way to group the poems, and nothing better came to mind.

"A Migrant's Late Breakfast"- For years I debated whether to include this poem with the County Road poems, as it seemed to stand on its own as a story poem. But in the end, I decided it fit after all. The hitcher here was apparently one of the "Chosin Few," the Marines who endured the horrible winter fighting around the Chosin Reservoir during the Korean War.

"Noon at the Wood County Fair: 1982"- Those of you who are old enough may recall that the early 1980s was a particularly rough time for farmers, a desultory mood presented at this county fair.

"An Old Lineman Near the Wood County Home"- This poem bounced around in my head for nearly 20 years before I was able to write it. After grad school, I considered becoming a telephone lineman back in Ohio. Linemen used to say that you could vaguely hear the voices buzzing in the old analog phone lines. At one time, every Ohio county had home for the aged. I lived for a while on a farm near this one.

THE WIDE PROSPECT

"LOOKING THE OTHER WAY"- This poem suggested itself as a title poem of something, though I could hardly have known at the time the ways in which my life would shift direction. This walk took place in October of 2006 during my first ever trip to California. The walkabout lasted for nearly eight hours as I waited for the long, multi-stop red-eye back to Maine. I hated the wait, but neither did I wish it to end. The poem is meant to capture a door ajar, each bit of my walk bumped the door a bit more. Not merely about the images of San Francisco in the poem, but already the beyond. I felt for the first time that pull of the Pacific.

"GUEST WORKER"- This poem emerged from conversations with a hotel waitress in Saipan. It is more or less her story, one that was all too common.

"A SONG TO THE MOON AT THE EDGE OF THE PHILIPPINE SEA"- On a long flight to Guam, on my way to Saipan, I heard for the first time the incredible aria from Dvorak's opera *Rusalka*. I could not let go of the words or the music as I tried to soak in the phenomenon that is Saipan. Through the years, the story turned over and over in me, the longing for what is not. Throughout Micronesia, but particularly in Saipan, one feels the clash of the old and the new in ways that are dislocating and even heartbreaking, the product of a shrinking world and even shrinking time, complicated by the waves of centuries-long colonial dominance. Some sort of universal longing lives in all of that history. The quoted lines in italics near the end of the poem are borrowed from Jarrell's "The Sick Naught."

"BIKINI"- The displacement of the Bikini Islanders during the nuclear testing in the post-war period, and their subsequent mistreatment, was heartbreaking and wanton in its cruelty. The specter remains. There are more historical references here than I normally employ. The Marshallese have a legend of a man who, out of envy, built his brother a canoe of ironwood, a wood denser than water, hoping to drown him. It's an old story, as they say.

"A CHILD OF A SOLDIER FROM THE WAR"- Being one of those whose parents lived through the Great Depression and World

173

War II has left its mark in more ways than I can begin to fathom. This poem emerged from a visit to Hawaii, including a trip to the U.S.S. Arizona Memorial.

"The Raft Boys of Majuro"- The Marshallese are master builders and paddlers of outrigger canoes. As in most cultures, play is often more than just play.

"At the Ruins of Nan Madol"- Nan Madol is a mysterious, ancient water city built among the mangrove shallows off the island of Pohnpei. *Ketieu* is a red-flowered plant said to have the power to ward off ghosts. *Pahi* were stones brought from a distant island. There were always 333 of them, one for each of the soldier guardians of Nan Madol, and they were held to ward off the powers of evil or war.

"1870, A Missionary Dreams Perhaps of Poetry"- This poem is a little harder to explain. The layers of various episodes of colonization dot the islands of Micronesia. What started as a picture of a ruined chapel got me to wondering what sort of impression the island of Pohnpei would have made on a missionary from snowy New England. Before I knew it, I was writing a poem.

"In the Belly of Ala Moana"- Ala Moana (meaning "path to the sea" in Hawai'ian) became, at least to me, a perverse name of an enormous, enclosed shopping mall in Honolulu. From the outside, the place resembles an old General Motors tank plant from WW II. On the inside, it was a dizzying array of lights and trendy shops and kiosks crowded with high-speed shoppers. I had intended to take a shortcut through the mall to meet a friend for lunch. Thirty minutes later I was still trying to find a way out. Another myth of Paradise.

Cantare to the Haunts of Power

"In the Matter of A.M. Galinova"- I originally conceived this poem as being written in the voice of a dead political prisoner, but gradually the voice of the interrogator began to assert itself. Galinova speaks only through the file and through the interrogator's memory. Although these characters are Russian, I wanted to capture some of the ethos common to all totalitarian views and practices of the world. Alas, no one seems to have a monopoly in such matters.

"Tulagi"- Tulagi was an island off Guadalcanal. The man in the poem was wounded in a battle there. The dream of the polar bear came from a fragment of overheard conversation in a coffee shop. *Poets must be dangerous listeners.*

"To J. Robert Oppenheimer, September 4, 1983"- Robert Oppenheimer seemed one of the more tortured individuals in our history. He had just been profiled on NPR as I left for my evening walk across the fields in Mercer, Maine.

"Eight Lost Photos by Andre Kertèsz"- Another series with a long gestation. For years I've admired the photography of Kertèsz; maybe it's something in my Hungarian blood. At any rate, I imagined some photos he might have taken across the 20th Century. The pickelhaube was the bizarre, spiked helmet worn by German and Austrian soldiers. Edward Teller really did lose his foot in a streetcar accident in Munich. The Vanilla Revolution refers to the brief reign of the Communists in Hungary following World War I. Apparently, the communes produced great quantities of vanilla ice cream. Teller's family home was confiscated by the revolutionary soldiers.

"A Scene from a War"- *Attack and Retreat* was an Italian movie with American actors (notably a young Peter Falk) about Italian troops fighting in the Ukraine. One of its more wrenching scenes sparked this poem.

"Leaving Hungnam: December 24, 1950"- Somehow, this little vignette crept into the collection. It probably got started many years ago. The story of the withdrawal of the First Marine Division from the area of the Chosin Reservoir was horrific enough, but there is always another layer to every story. Hungnam was the port of evacuation, which, of course, needed to be destroyed afterwards.

"Here, There, and Away"- I saw this Winslow Homer show following the funeral of my godfather. In Maine, if you are not a native, you are "from away." Well, that all depends on where you've stood, as my fellow Midwesterner Terry Plunkett grasped so well.

"Winter Laundry"- A friend once accused me of writing "drive-by poetry." He may have had a point; it seems I notice a lot of things while driving. Some of those things became prose poems like this one.

"*Lavarando nel Cuore Solo*"- I wrote this poem as a tribute to my dear friend and occasional collaborator, the artist Leonard Craig. I was honored to have it read at his memorial. The title translates as "working in the heart alone," a topic of many of our conversations about the lives of poets and painters.

Waiting Places

"ADVENT AT THE PORT OF GALILEE"- This poem begins a selection of Advent poems, which I have written now for 54 years. The poems always treat Advent as a season of hopefulness, which as I tell people is about 15 degrees south of hope. In this case I was sitting in a restaurant in Galilee, Rhode Island, watching a dragger riding the evening tide home. As usual, an occasion for pondering the permutations of remaining hopeful.

"TRUE AND UNTRUE AT CHRISTMAS"- "True and Untrue" is the title of a Norse folk tale in which two brothers have those names. That tale had fascinated me since childhood, and I had many aborted efforts of using it in a poem through the years. The moral of this version may be don't invite a poet to your home at Christmas.

"THE TRACE OF HOPE AT LOCK 29"- Lock 29 on the old Ohio & Erie Canal was an aqueduct that raised the canal boats above the bending stretch of the Cuyahoga River at the village of Peninsula, Ohio. Remnants of the old lock remain, and I have visited many times. For some reason, Lock 29 called to me as a site for this Advent poem. You might think it an odd place to seek hopefulness, but I have found all such places to appear odd choices, at least at first.

Matters of the Heart

"A STORY ABOUT LOVE AT TENANT'S HARBOR"- Some friend or other once told me that love poems are impossible, that if you start with that premise, oddly enough you may be able to write them. This story poem was one that just happened in front of me as I was pulling my kayak out of the water.

"IN A CHILDREN'S GALLERY"- This poem is a sort of love poem stopping short. The two lines in italics were stolen from Randall Jarrell's poem "Children Selecting Books in a Library."

"RICORDI"- A sequence of these poems were first written one each day in the winter of 2002. They were printed with color reproductions of paintings by my friend the renowned artist Leonard Craig. 27 Ricordi in Winter was a private edition of 100 signed and numbered copies. I made up the nine-line form for the Ricordi, a word that came to me from a series of Leonard's paintings done years before. He assured me that the term in Italian translates as "especially heartfelt remembrances." I continue to write them.

About the Author

David Adams is a poet living in Burton, Ohio. For many years he was a wandering laborer, academic and technical writer, finally returning home in 2011.

Hope as a Construction is his 11th collection of poems. His prose memoir, *Casual Labor,* was published by Blue Shale Books in 2021. With Linda Wagner-Martin, he edited *Over West: Selected Writings of Frederick Eckman* (1999. National Poetry Foundation). He is also the author of *COPE: A Technical Writing Guide for Engineers, 4th Ed*. 2021, University of New Haven.

As a librettist, David collaborated with the composer Dawn Sonntag to complete in 2022 *Clara: A Life and Death in Shadow,* an opera in three acts about the life of Clara Haber.

Books by Bottom Dog Press

Harmony Series

Hope as a Construction, by David Adams, 182 pgs., $18
Baltic Amber in a Chest: Poems, by Clarissa Jakobsons, 104 pgs., $16
Choices: Three Novellas by Annabel Thomas, 176 pgs., $18
Pottery Town Blues, by Karen Kotrba, 128 pgs., $16
The Pears: Poems, by Larry Smith, 66 pgs, $15
Cycling Through Columbine, by JRW Case, 258 pgs., $18
Without a Plea, by Jeff Gundy, 96 pgs, $16
Taking a Walk in My Animal Hat, by Charlene Fix, 90 pgs, $16
Earnest Occupations, by Richard Hague, 200 pgs, $18
Pieces: A Composite Novel, by Mary Ann McGuigan, 250 pgs, $18
Crows in the Jukebox: Poems, by Mike James, 106 pgs, $16
Portrait of the Artist as a Bingo Worker: A Memoir, by Lori Jakiela, 216 pgs, $18
The Thick of Thin: A Memoir, by Larry Smith, 238 pgs, $18
Cold Air Return: A Novel, by Patrick Lawrence O'Keeffe, 390 pgs, $20
Flesh and Stones: A Memoir, by Jan Shoemaker, 176 pgs, $18
Waiting to Begin: A Memoir, by Patricia O'Donnell, 166 pgs, $18
And Waking: Poems, by Kevin Casey, 80 pgs, $16
Both Shoes Off: Poems, by Jeanne Bryner, 112 pgs, $16
Abandoned Homeland: Poems, by Jeff Gundy, 96 pgs, $16
Stolen Child: A Novel, by Suzanne Kelly, 338 pgs, $18

Bottom Dog Press, Inc.
P.O. Box 425 /Huron, Ohio 44839
http://smithdocs.net